Shafted

Shafted:
The Media, the Miners' Strike & the Aftermath

Edited by Granville Williams

CAMPAIGN FOR PRESS AND BROADCASTING FREEDOM

Contents

List of illustrations
following page 64

Shafted: The Media, the Miners' Strike and the Aftermath
Published to mark the 25th anniversary of the miners' strike March 2009
by the *Campaign for Press and Broadcasting Freedom*
2nd Floor, Vi and Garner Smith House, 23 Orford Road, Walthamstow,
London E17 9NL
Edited by Granville Williams

ISBN 978 1 898240 05 1

Design and production: Roger Huddle
Printed by the Aldgate Press
Units 5&6, Gunthorpe Street Workshops
3 Gunthorpe Street, London E1 7RQ

Cover: North Selby NUM banner

Andrew Turner, the son of a miner from West Lothian, designed the North
Selby NUM banner. The powerful statement about the role of the media,
police and government, which the banner forcefully expresses, made British
Coal management uneasy. On pit 'open days' when miners' families and the
public could visit the colliery the management would not allow the banner
to be displayed.

There were five pits in the Selby Coalfield, which cost £1.3 billion to
develop: Wistow, Stillingfleet, North Selby, Riccall and Whitemoor. There
were two long tunnels driven right through the coalfield, called trunk roads
or spine roads, and they were each 11 miles long.

Each pit was connected to the spine roads and all the coal was delivered to
them and then came to the surface - not up traditional shafts but up drifts
to the surface - at a central point at Gascoigne Wood. Gascoigne Wood did
not produce coal itself but handled all the coal from the Selby Coalfield.
The Selby coalfield finally closed in 2003 leaving vast quantities of coal
behind.

Foreword
Tony Benn

We can now look back on the miners' strike and see it much more clearly. Mrs Thatcher launched a major counter-revolution against democracy when she came to power and she did it by attacking the three pillars of the Labour movement.

The first pillar was the trade union movement which had founded the Labour Party and campaigned for socialism. The miners being the strongest trade union, she took them on first, describing the most skilled and courageous workers in Britain as 'the enemy within' and releasing the police and the army against their picket lines which were to defend their jobs and the industry.

She also strangled local government and began a programme of privatisation to reverse the gains that had been made by Labour's reforms to put the basic industries under public control.

Now, twenty five years later this country still has 300 years of coal reserves under its territory, not enough miners to dig it, and is engaged in wars for energy in Iraq and Afghanistan.

Her campaign, which was brutal in its effect on whole communities, can now be seen to have been an act of incredible economic lunacy, for which we are already paying a price.

During the miners' strike Women Against Pit Closures played a phenomenal role and Arthur Scargill warned that this was only the first attack on the working class and that if the NUM went down everyone else would be vulnerable – and how right he was.

The legacy that Thatcherism left included legislation against trade unionism that makes it almost illegal to engage in its proper and normal processes. And New Labour never repealed that legislation, with the result that today trade unionism is hardly mentioned except when there is the occasional strike and the unions are blamed for undermining the economy.

But today who believes for a moment that it has been the unions that have been responsible for this massive economic crisis? That responsibility must be accepted by those who planned the unregulated economy that is now at breaking point.

It is to the future that we must look, for the present crisis is a deep political crisis as well as an economic one. We know from the experience of the pre-war slump that such a crisis can trigger a national government which would exclude choice from the electorate and could even create the conditions in which the fascists could reappear, then under Mosley, and now linked to the BNP.

We have got to see that the nation's energy resources, and its transport, water and banks, are returned to public ownership so that we can plan a recovery with the same determination that any nation plans for war.

That was how in 1945 Labour rescued a bankrupt economy and set it up with the NHS, the Welfare State and all the services that made life tolerable for working people for the first time in our history.

Labour and the left must now come together with a similar programme and campaign for it relentlessly, knowing that there will be massive public support from those who are going to suffer greatly and who may even be made to suffer, as victims often are, for crimes they did not commit.

Acknowledgements & thanks

It has been a real pleasure to plan and edit this book.
That might sound odd when the subject is how the media
reported the defeat of a strike and the destruction of an
industry, but contained in this book are important stories
and issues which a new generation needs to know about,
and others to be reminded of. All of the contributors
to this book responded very positively to the request to
contribute, and I am really grateful to them for their efforts.
I particularly want to thank Janina Struk who at short notice
filled the gap on photography and the miners' strike in
the book. Michael Bailey, Nicholas Jones, Pete Lazenby
and Julian Petley have been enthusiastic supporters of the
book and provided valuable suggestions. I hope all the
contributors think the end product is one they are pleased
to be associated with.
Thanks to Mick Gosling for suggesting the title and Paul
Herrmann for putting me in touch with Andy Boag.
This book is published by the Campaign for Press and
Broadcasting Freedom (CPBF) and members of its National
Council, particularly Barry White and Larry Herman, have
also provided valuable advice and support - indeed several
Council members are also contributors.
Finally many thanks to Roger Huddle for advice and
handling the design and printing of the book. Thanks also
for the following union donations (as we went to press) to
support the book's publication: BECTU, Yorkshire NUM,
UCATT and several UNISON branches.
GW

Introduction: Look back in anger
Granville Williams

The Czech writer Milan Kundera suggests we are 'separated from the past (even from the past only a few seconds ago) by two forces that instantly go to work and cooperate: the force of forgetting (which erases) and the force of memory (which transforms)...'[1] A traveller returning to the Dearne Valley in South Yorkshire after a quarter of a century would not recognise it. The forces of erasure have been rampant. The only reminders of the string of pits which once sustained employment for 60,000-70,000 miners and a distinctive way of life in mining towns and villages scattered across the Dearne Valley, such as Brampton, Denaby, Grimethorpe, Wath and Wombwell, are their names on some of the roundabouts on the new road, the Dearne Valley Parkway, which now crosses the terrain where they once were. The Alamo, the miners' own name for their picketing redoubt, stood at Cortonwood Colliery throughout the 1984-85 strike. Now a supermarket stands in its place. It was the bombshell announcement on 1 March 1984 by the National Coal Board (NCB) area director, George Hayes, to close the pit on 6 April 1984 which triggered the epic industrial struggle. Eighty miners from the closed Elsecar colliery had recently moved to Cortonwood, where an investment of over £1 million pounds had recently been made, on the understanding that the pit had five years' life in it still.

The photographer Andy Boag is on the side of the force of memory in his inspired project to locate the sites of the closed pits in Yorkshire and to seek out men who worked in them to have their photos taken. He explains:

'The Conservative government was so keen to eradicate any physical traces of the collieries on the landscape that very little remains (if anything) of the old workings on the twenty-fifth anniversary of the miners' strike. In another twenty five years there will be less still.

I visited the sites of collieries in Yorkshire that closed in the 5-year period following the strike to photograph and interview a miner who worked at each of them. Each location photograph was taken where the shafts were sunk, the site of the original pit yard. It is not so much about the strike itself, more the physical and social legacy of a once-massive industry all but wiped out in a decade.

Two significant things that struck me during the course of the project were firstly how little physical remains of the collieries still existed - in some cases nothing at all. Sometimes it would be impossible to pin point the colliery landmarks even in the company of someone who had worked there for 35 years. Secondly, whilst some sites had been redeveloped as business parks, many were just razed to the ground with little attempt to provide alternative employment opportunities for the local community.'

Sid Bailey (fig 1) stands where Cortonwood pit stood until its closure in October 1985.

The same impulse to document and remind people of the scale and impact of mining motivates Rachel Poole, the daughter of a former miner at Bentley Colliery, Doncaster, in her 'Pin The Pits' campaign which wants Ordnance Survey maps to carry a half-pit wheel symbol to designate former pits in regenerated mining areas like the Dearne Valley.

In 1947 when the 958 largest pits were taken into public ownership coal was the primary source for 90 per cent of the UK's energy and over 700,000 men worked in the industry. The growing use of oil over the next two decades led to a steady contraction in the number of pits and many displaced miners, mainly from Scotland and the North-East, relocated to the rich central coalfields of Yorkshire, Nottingham and the Midlands as pits closed in their areas. At the start of the miners' strike in 1984 170 collieries remained employing 196,000 miners.

The forces unleashed during the bitterly contested year-long strike have been summarised by former Scottish miner, Joe Owens, reflecting on the calendar year of the strike and the title of George Orwell's dystopian novel, *1984*:

'In Tory Britain in 1984, the experience of the miners' strike provided a contemporary glimpse of the immense power and potential brutality of the existing state machine when it swung into service on behalf of power.

The union was infiltrated and attempts made to destabilise it financially and organisationally. The apparat of the judiciary and the legislature assiduously pursued every legal avenue, however obscure, to break the union. Basic civil rights of assembly, freedom of movement and freedom from arbitrary arrest were curtailed, even suspended. The right to work, seemingly inapplicable in the argument against pit closures and redundancies, was upheld with all the rigour and vigour of the law, if it meant another man through the picket line.

For the police and their highly-trained, well-equipped and sophisticated riot squads, breaking the union had a more prosaic quality. The image of the thin blue line was replaced with that of the beefy paramilitary with the thick black truncheon and riot shield. Illusions of the police as just another emergency service were literally beaten out of miners and their families in scenes of quite sickening brutality.' [2]

The *Justice for Mineworkers Campaign* points out, 'During the strike 20,000 people were injured or hospitalised (including NUM President Arthur Scargill). 200 served time in prison or custody. Two miners, David Jones and Joe Green, were killed on picket lines, three died digging for coal during the winter and 966 were sacked.' [3]

Another account of the strike, GB84 by David Peace, a 'fiction based on fact', also captures the ways in which the sacrifices and solidarity of the striking miners were undermined by government, police and media. It is a savage, unrelenting portrayal of the militarisation of the police, the surveillance and wire-tapping of NUM activists, and the stresses and strains on the miners and their families as they grappled with financial hardship. Disused airfields are reopened as police barracks, mining villages ringed with police, roadblocks established restricting civilian movement, and Yorkshire mining areas seen as occupied territory in a state of siege.

But the strike also unleashed other positive, creative forces of socialist and trade union solidarity, nationally and internationally, in support of the miners and, most strikingly, the emergence of Women Against Pit Closures. And twenty-five years on we can see ever more clearly what was distinctive about the miners' struggle at the time. Geoffrey Goodman, then the industrial editor of the *Daily Mirror*, pointed out the dispute was 'unique in terms of conventional industrial conflict. It was not about the pay packet; it was not about working conditions, hours of work, or even in the normal sense, a traditional conflict with management...the future of work was at the core of it. To remove a pit from a mining community is to snap the lifeline to a job'. [4]

From the end of the strike up to 1990 the number of pits was cut back to 73 with production concentrated in the most productive. The final blow was the calculated political decision by the Conservative government to privatise the electricity supply industry. The then Energy Secretary, Cecil Parkinson, explained in his memoirs the strategy was simple: break the monopoly of coal and energy and privatise them to destroy the economic and political power of the

National Union of Mineworkers.[5] The power industry was privatised in 1990 and on 13 October 1992 Michael Heseltine announced his pit closure programme. But in stark contrast to 1984-85 the Conservative government plans unleashed a wave of popular protest. The Women Against Pit Closures played an important role with pit camps at Markham Main and Grimethorpe, and at the front door of Heseltine's DTI offices in London. Newspapers which were relentlessly hostile during the year-long strike now supported the miners and 200,000 people joined a TUC march in protest. But the closures went ahead, followed by the rapid privatisation of the rest of the mines in 1994. The Conservative strategy created a rigged market through the 'dash for gas', the import of heavily subsidised coal and the use of nuclear power, and the result was further closures. By early 2008 the deep-mined UK coal industry in the nations and regions had shrunk to six pits with the closure of Tower Colliery in January. UK Coal run Kellingley in West Yorkshire, Thoresby and Welbeck in Nottinghamshire, and Daw Mill near Coventry; Hargreaves own Maltby Colliery in South Yorkshire; and Powerfuel Hatfield Colliery near Doncaster in South Yorkshire. In total fewer than 4000 miners work in these remaining pits.

Twenty-five years after the epic struggle of 1984-85 and the subsequent pit closure programme of 1992-93, the pain and anger in mining communities at the devastation and suffering inflicted remains acute. Films like *Brassed Off* (1996) and *Billy Elliot* (2000) vividly conveyed the hardship, disruption and demoralisation in coal field communities following the politically driven closures. In *Brassed Off*, set in the film in Grimley but based on the real village of Grimethorpe, the brass band leader Danny, played by Peter Postlethwaite, struggles to sustain the band's morale against the backcloth of threatened pit closure. As the coal mine itself is finally closed, the band reaches the final at the Royal Albert Hall in London, but after winning the competition Danny refuses to accept the trophy stating that it's only human beings that matter and not music or the trophy. The 'government has systematically destroyed an entire industry. Our industry. And not just our industry - our communities, our homes, our lives. All in the name of "progress". And for a few lousy bob'. Once the pit went Grimethorpe saw its population fall by more than a fifth to less than 4,000 in the next 11 years, ill-health rise to twice the national average, house prices drop to 80 per cent below, and a sharp increase in vandalism, drug-taking and crime. Only now is the village beginning slowly to revive as part of the regeneration efforts across the Dearne Valley.

David Douglass, for years an activist in the Yorkshire NUM and branch secretary at Hatfield Colliery in Stainforth near Doncaster, captures the devastating impact on Barnsley, where in the 1960s within a fifteen-mile radius of the town centre seventy pits operated, but by 1994 none survived:

'The shock of that transformation, and the manner by which it was imposed, still resonates through those communities. It is as if a great machine suddenly fell silent. In the pubs and clubs the old lads will still tell the tale and draw on their immense reserves of humour and wit. On the weekend streets the young'uns will still strut their stuff, but something at the heart has died. There is a collective bereavement here which is still raw. Grown men, who have faced great hardship with courage, can now be moved to tears while reflecting on the last two decades and its impact on them, their families, and their communities. There were more than just job losses.' [6]

Speaking to former miners about the strike it is extraordinary how, after twenty-five years, anger and bitterness well up about the Tory government, the bully-boy tactics of the riot police, and the bias in the media. The wound is still raw and pressing. The strength of outrage against the actions taken by Thatcher's government during the strike, and the axe subsequently wielded by John Major's government, is also still palpable across all sections of society.

On July 13 2008 the *Mail on Sunday* carried a report that Margaret Thatcher would be given the rare honour of a state funeral. The proposal triggered widespread, bitterly hostile reactions from people who had suffered at the sharp end of Thatcher's policies. The following evening Eddie Mair on BBC's PM radio news invited listeners to give their views on the topic. Up to July 20 PM received 156 responses. Eleven of these made general comments, the same number were removed for breaking the BBC's house rules, four supported the idea and the rest were hostile, often savagely so. John Kiddey's comment was typical: 'Her legacy could not be more divisive; she destroyed whole communities - mining, shipbuilding, iron and steel, creating the selfish loadsamoney society of the eighties and, thence, the amoral society we have today.' Weaved into the listeners' comments was her role in the 1984-85 miners' strike which 'laid waste the mining communities' and left them 'destitute'. Another suggested: 'A great idea to take her to the land of King Arthur, Barnsley and lay her to rest deep inside the mines she managed to destroy!' Dave Brown's cartoon in *The Independent* with six miners as the pall bearers carrying Mrs T. wrapped in a union jack to a refuse lorry, with a tearful Gordon Brown as the funeral director walking behind, captured this pervasive mood exactly (fig 2). The press reports about the state funeral also inspired the play *Maggie's End* by Ed Waugh and Trevor Wood which premiered at the Gala theatre in Durham in October 2008, with sponsorship from the NUM North East area, RMT, UNITE and the GMB, and will move to London in April 2009 to mark the 25th anniversary of the strike.

In autumn 2008 the lax regulation and financial excesses of banks led to a government bail-out with billions of pounds of taxpayers' money. A letter by Chris Waller in *The Observer* (5 October 2008) highlighted the bitter disparity between the treatment meted out to the miners, compared with the extravagant state support for the bankers:

'I recall no weeping and gnashing of teeth in the City
when the coal mining industry was devastated by the ill-
considered application of a flawed economic ideology.
The consequence of that arrogant idiocy now leaves us
dependent for the major part of this country's energy
supplies on sources over which we have no control.'

We need to remember what the real economic and social
costs of the destruction of the coal industry have been. Dave
Feickert, national research officer for the NUM from 1983-
93, put the costs at between £28.5 -£33 billion, and believes
'the horrendous damage to mining communities will take
at least two generations to heal, notwithstanding the work
of the Coalfields Regeneration Trusts and the Coalfield
Communities Campaign. Never', he writes, 'has there been
such a wilful destruction of so many individual communities,
of such a vast amount of productive public capital, or of a
nation's strategic energy resource.' [7]

Yes, we should look back in anger, and hold fast to the
force of memory.

Notes

1   Milan Kundera, *The Curtain*, HarperCollins, 2007.

2   Joe Owens, *Miners 1984-1994: A Decade of Endurance*, Polygon, 1995, pp
7-8.

3   The *National Justice for Mineworkers Campaign* at
http://www.justiceformineworkers.org.uk/

4   Gooffrey Goodman, *The Miners' Strike*, Pluto Press, 1985, p15.

5   Cecil Parkinson, *Right At The Centre London*, Weidenfeld & Nicholson,
1992.

6   David Douglass, *Strike, Not The End Of The Story*, National Coal Mining
Museum, 2005.

7   Dave Feickert, 'Arthur was right by instinct,' *The Guardian*, 11.02.2004.

Trade union solidarity and the miners' strike

Trade union solidarity with the miners took many forms (fig 3). In Birmingham, for example, Paul Mackney, Vice President of Birmingham Trades Council during 1984-85 and chair of the support group, published an account of the work of Birmingham trades unionists to support the miners, in which he pointed out that the support committees that emerged throughout Britain involved 'more people at a greater pitch of activity over a lengthier period than any other campaign in the history of the labour movement. It would not be an exaggeration to say that it represented the biggest civilian mobilisation in Britain since the Second World War'.[1]

The railwaymen: Geoff Revell [2]

The NUM and the rail unions – the NUR, TSSA and ASLEF – met at the NUR headquarters throughout the dispute. The NUR and ASLEF also met monthly under its Rail Federation of Unions where the miners' strike was top of the agenda. Throughout the year-long strike not one ton of coal moved by rail, though not without incident, and wherever attempts to move coal by rail were made, solidarity action took place.
Before the strike the giant Orgreave coking plant was entirely serviced by rail, with coal slack moved in, reprocessed into coke and then transported to industrial sites such as the steel works at Scunthorpe. Tinsley NUR and ASLEF branches met with the area NUM and agreed that if the miners mounted a picket over the road bridge at Treeton the rail workers would refuse to move train in or out of the site. Gerry Hitchen of the NUR was involved at the time:

'I turned up for work that morning at half past seven. There was absolute chaos. There was everyone there. There were top managers. There was British Transport Police, civil police. The driver of the first train was prepared to take the coke train out and even the guard was prepared to take the train out but the shunter, a guy called Billy Burns, wouldn't open the points. Everyone got involved. And as a consequence of that the union's Local Department Committee came up and gave a bollocking to the driver and guard. From that day on not one single train moved in or out of Orgreave coking plant'.

As a result of this sympathetic action by railway workers the NCB had to bring the coal by road which resulted in the bloody battle of Orgreave. However in some areas, where the strike was less solid and membership divided, difficulties were bound to arise.

Two very different stories of solidarity action by railway workers for the miners, at Coalville in Leicestershire and Shirebrook in Derbyshire, reveal the dilemmas faced by trade unionists in the middle of this great struggle.

Coalville

The Mantle Lane rail depot at Coalville was in the heart of the Leicestershire coalfields, serving three national power stations: Drakelow, Didcot and Rugeley. From the outset of the strike almost all of the miners of the Leicestershire union, some 2,500, worked in defiance of the national union. However a handful of loyal miners supported their leadership and joined the strike. They were dubbed 'the dirty thirty'. The NUR members at the Coalville depot, numbering 160, took solidarity action in support of the miners who had joined the strike.

On 3rd April 1984 the Coalville NUR members refused to handle coal from anywhere in Leicestershire. When three guards were sent home, their fellow workers walked out in

support. After one week on strike a settlement was reached, the NUR members would allow the movement of coal from a local privately owned open-cast mine in return for allowing surplus rail workers to perform duties other than moving coal. As a result virtually all of the coal worked from the NCB pits in Leicestershire was blacked and for the first three months of the strike was stockpiled in huge heaps around the Coalville depot, testimony to the productivity of the working pits, but also the solidarity of the railway workers.
As the strike continued the attacks on the miners became more vicious, a virtual national police force had evolved and Thatcher was bent on using them to break the strike. This situation gave the local BR management the confidence to move against the Coalville rail workers. On 7th July the regional operating manager ordered all the rail workers to resume normal working in twenty-four hours or face disciplinary action. Local branches of NUR and ASLEF met and decided to stand firm. The railway bosses responded by a lock out which lasted two months. Members of Derbyshire branches of NUR and ASLEF struck for twenty-four hours in support of their colleagues at Coalville, closing the east coast main line railway. Worried that pay negotiations, together with the Coalville dispute, might escalate the strike BR ordered the management at Coalville to back off.
With pay negotiations settled the attitude of the BR hardened again. In late September a new area manager was appointed with instructions to sort out Coalville depot. He announced that if the rail workers did not return to normal working by 1st October then the Coalville depot would be closed down. On the same day as the announcement British Transport police raided the homes of seven railwaymen, including the local branch secretary, under suspicion of stealing railway property. Three were sacked after several items of 'railway property' were found consisting of soap, cleaning rags and a few batteries. More intimidation was to come. In mid-

December 1984, when the NCB became desperate to break the miners once and for all, it became even more important to break the Coalville blockade. The local BR management tried to put pressure, in the way of a bribe, on signalman Edwin Hampton to make him break ranks and take part in the movement of coal from a local pit to Drakelow power station. When he flatly refused he was declared 'mentally unstable' and moved from the signal box. The then Rail Federation of the NUR and ASLEF responded by calling strikes at eleven depots covering the London Midland and Eastern regions of BR. Then on 17th January 1985 a twenty-four hour strike was held in freezing winter conditions of all workers on the London Midland North-east regions of BR with the threat of an all-out national strike. Faced with this the BR bosses caved in and the 'mentally unstable' Edwin Hampton returned to his signal-box.

Shirebrook

The coal depot at Shirebrook, north Derbyshire, which straddled the Nottinghamshire border, was also a site of bitter conflict. The situation here was more complicated than Coalville but equally intimidating. Close to the Nottinghamshire coal fields, one of the most hotly contested areas of the strike, Shirebrook depot serviced the nearby Shirebrook and Warsop collieries as well as eleven other mines in the area., operating a 'merry-go-round' service for the important electricity generating stations in the Trent valley: Ratcliffe-on-Soar, West Burton, High Marnham and Cottam. Though the men at the local pits were supporters of the strike, in the surrounding countryside of north Nottinghamshire miners were working normally. Loyalties were divided at the rail depot, with many men of the local NUR branch having family connections with working miners. Local reluctance to show solidarity with striking miners was deep with the Shirebrook branch secretary calling for the NUM to ballot nationally.

As a result only a handful of NUR and ASLEF men initially obeyed the directive from their own Executive Committees. From April 1984 through to the end of May six local meetings were held by local union officials calling for the men to act. When these efforts failed NUR and ASLEF General Secretaries, Jimmy Knapp and Ray Buckton addressed joint meetings in an effort to get the members behind their own union decisions. They went to any meeting called to address the concerns. Knapp recalled speaking to a rail worker who had two sons still digging coal. As a result of these meetings a vote of the Shirebrook men came out narrowly in favour of supporting the miners. By mid June, a third of the guards and half of the drivers blacked coal movements. Further local lobbying by the NUR and ASLEF leaderships persuaded more men to join the action and by the height of the strike more than two-thirds of the guards and three-quarters of the drivers took part. It became clear to the enemies of the miners and trade union solidarity that this state of affairs should not continue. The Nottinghamshire miners were digging the coal out but the rail workers were not moving it

In July, when the NCB embarked on an effort to force the miners at the local pits to get back to work the bosses turned their attention to Shirebrook. British Transport Police, in full riot gear with horses and dogs, were deployed in the depot. The police stopped and interviewed railwaymen on their way to work and set up in the very room the men used to book on. At the same time management at the depot suddenly refused to book on anyone who refused to 'work normally', in other words to handle coal, and sent those who refused home. Those who were refused booking on had 'Code 22' entered on their payslips which meant they were officially declared to be on strike and therefore not entitled to tax rebates. Management put up propaganda posters showing coal being moved by road and free visits were offered to the railwaymen to see the lorry convoys carrying coal entering power stations, coal that was once moved by rail. Guards at Shirebrook and Warsop were phoned at home by managers who cajoled and threatened to get them to move coal. In September a 24-hour strike was called to support the Shirebrook workers. The constant effort by the rail unions leadership to hold some kind of line at Shirebrook went on throughout the dispute. By the new year, as the NUM resolve began to weaken, only 50% of the workers at Shirebrook were supporting any kind of action. The near blockade of the movement of coal continued throughout the strike.

Elsewhere support for the strike by members in Scotland, South Wales, the North West, South Yorkshire and Kent was total. Railworkers joined with other workers throughout the country and abroad to try to ensure that the miners and their families would not be starved into submission. NUR union branches 'twinned' with miners' branches, joined the picket lines, held socials to raise funds and pressed the TUC to give greater support. As the strike wore on and it became clear that the government had set out deliberately to smash the NUM, then lay waste the mining communities, many rank and file members of other unions knew what a defeat for the miners would mean for them.

A night to remember

It was not just the traditional organised working class that rallied round the miners' cause, and not just in industrial areas. There were many among the radicalised middle class, from the so-called 1968 generation, who were becoming horrified at the transformation of society wrought by Margaret Thatcher and saw the dispute as a battle in the class war in which you had to take sides.

It was only ten years, after all, since to the astonishment of the political class a general election had been won by Labour, in a far less polarised political environment, on a wave of support for the miners against the Tory government of Edward

Heath. Now, though the government and Coal Board were
determined to win, and the propaganda against the miners
was intense, there was still a swell of support among middle-
of-the road citizens that their treatment was unfair and the
destruction of coalmining was an affront to Britain's industrial
culture.

As well as the collectors that became a ubiquitous sight rat-
tling buckets outside stores and supermarkets in even the
most upmarket areas, there were hundreds of branches in
white collar and professional unions that expressed their
support directly, by linking with and visiting pit village communities and hosting the miners and their families at fundraising events.

You could not identify a more petit bourgeois collective of
workers than the London Freelance Branch (LFB) of the
National Union of Journalists (NUJ), consisting entirely of
self-employed writers, broadcasters and photographers. But
the LFB 'adopted' the community of the Fitzwilliam and
Kinsley drift mine villages in West Yorkshire and maintained
a high level of activity in its support right up to the end.
There turned out to be a common sense of purpose between
the movement of miners' wives, who demonstrated such
confidence as political campaigners, and the feminists at that
time carving out positions in the trade union movement.
LFB's activities were based strongly on this connection, with
all-women delegations going from London to the villages,
driving up their old bangers loaded with carloads of food and
household supplies, and miners' wives coming to speak at
meetings in London.

The LFB raised a lot of money for the cause, peaking with a
memorable benefit gig at Christmas 1984. The branch hired
the main hall at the University of London Union (ULU) for
a show featuring the *Redskins*, a skinhead punk band individual members of which were in the Socialist Workers Party.
The Redskins were the SWP and Anti-Nazi League's answer to

the Fourskins and other Nazi skinhead bands. They produced an album called *Neither Washington Nor Moscow* – an SWP slogan at the time – and their singer was X Moore – Chris Moore, a music writer on NME and an active member of the NUJ. They had a lively following of leftwing kids, all skinheads togged out in tight faded jeans, white T-shirts, college boy jackets and boxing boots.

Unfortunately they also had virulent antagonists, in gangs of Nazi skinheads (similarly clad but in Doc Martens boots), and it was not unusual to see violent set-tos around their gigs. Intelligence of this state of affairs reached ULU managers on the day of the gig and they called LFB to tell them it was off. A branch officer rushed around to ask whether ULU rally wanted a few hundred angry *Redskins* fans around their building that night. But ULU's insurers had withdrawn their cover for the event and the only solution offered was for LFB to pay a one-off extra premium – and that was £1,000. The union had no choice but to pay and the gig went ahead.

It was a belting success. Just as the *Redskins* were winding up to their final number, their theme song 'Keep On Keeping On', one of the miners from Fitzwilliam came on stage and took the mike. 'I've come to London to say one thing,' he said. 'Metropolitan Police are scum of the earth'. The place went wild. The kids stormed into the street and attacked the university bookshop opposite. Every window was smashed and all books on display were liberated and offered for sale to bemused Christmas revellers going home that night on the underground.

But the union was covered. The event still made £3,000 for the miners' families of Fitzwilliam and Kinsley.

Solidarity in Hertfordshire:
Bernie Wooder and *Anne Page*
At the time of the strike Bernie Wooder was a SOGAT activist and former shop steward in the print union. He lived

(and stills lives) in Elstree and Boreham Wood, just outside
London in leafy Hertfordshire. His MP, Cecil Parkinson, was
one of the small group of Tory Cabinet ministers who ran the
Government's fight against the miners. Parkinson regarded
the strike as 'closer to revolution than a strike... much in the
nature of a Peasants' Revolt or a Luddite assault upon new
textile machinery, as well as a political attempt to humiliate
and perhaps destroy the Government'. [3]

Parkinson's views were not shared by all his constituents
and Bernie was part of a miners support group set up in the
town early in the winter of 1984. As with many other support groups it was a coalition of trade unionists, socialists and
community activists. They set up a weekly stall every Saturday outside the parish church of All Saints in Boreham Wood
High Street, where they collected food, clothes and toys for
striking miners and their families in Nottinghamshire.

Bernie recalls one occasion, in the early days, when they got a
visit from an over-enthusiastic Metropolitan police constable.
Telling the group to 'move on' he was quickly confronted
by the local rector (priest) who calmly, but firmly told the
young police constable that Bernie and the group were on
church property. 'Constable – you see that line on the pave-
ment there?' 'Yes Sir' came the response. 'Well everything
that happens on your side of that line is your business. On
this side it's mine and I have given full permission for them
to be here'. Embarrassed and chastised the representative of
law and order slinked away. 'An interesting conflict between
Church and State, where the cloth and collar triumphed,'
Bernie recalls.

Not all confrontations were so straightforward. When the
stall was visited by an elderly working class woman, she
received a warm welcome. Courtesy was repaid by the visitor
bearing her teeth, spitting on the food collected and swear-
ing. 'You are all effing commies' she shouted. 'Why don't you
go back to Russia?'

Bernie recalls another incident at the stall when a rather well dressed driver of either a Bentley or a Rolls parked nearby and came over to the stall and handed over a cheque (to their surprise and relief). 'We looked at the cheque and were gob-smacked – it was for £360 drawn on the Bank of Seychelles. Before leaving he shook hands with everyone, leaving the group with the clear 'keep it up!' Bernie recalls.

During the dispute, miners' supporters in both Elstree and Boreham Wood and Radlett (a smaller town nearby) were visited by striking miners from the Newstead Colliery Village and Annesley in Nottinghamshire. Some stayed at the home of Robin and Anne Page in Radlett (Robin was the Labour Party secretary of the Hertsmere Constituency). When a number of miners fell foul of the law and were arrested for various public order offences they secured the services of Paul Boateng, then a barrister, who acted in their defence. (Boateng later became an MP and the UK's first black Cabinet minister in May 2002 when he was appointed as Chief Secretary to the Treasury. An MP for Brent South from 1987 to 2005, he is the current British High Commissioner to South Africa.) She recalls that Paul asked if she could accommodate half a dozen Welsh miners whose case had been adjourned to the next day and had nowhere to stay. 'That evening we had about eight miners staying with us and were sleeping wherever they could find space in the house' recalls Anne. Anne also remembers that two miners from Nottinghamshire (Dave and Steve) stayed at their home for a few months, working with the miners' support group in St Albans, a few miles away. During the strike the group raised over £30,000. 'They collected every Saturday outside the Town Hall and got a lot of abuse, but tremendous support as well,' recalls Anne. 'They also met every Tuesday evening in the Beehive pub in St Albans to keep up-to-date with the miners' situation and to identify their most pressing needs.'

NALGO and the Miners' strike

In 1984 NALGO (the national and local government officers association) was Britain's fourth biggest union with over 750,000 members in local government, health and the nationalised utilities. It had supported the miners' strikes of 1972 and 1974 agreeing not to use the 1974 settlement as justification for their own pay claims.

In April 1984 the union's NEC donated £10,000 to the NUM's hardship fund and called on its districts and branches to hold workplace collections and make donations. NALGO branches set up miners' support groups (as did NALGO staff based in its London headquarters) and joined other groups set up by trades councils, Labour Party branches and other local organisations. 'Countless (NALGO) activists were involved in collecting money, food and household essentials, helping with holiday and Christmas parties for children, taking NUM fundraisers including women's support groups from the coalfields into their homes and generally doing anything and everything possible to help win the strike. The activists at (the June 1984) annual conference supported the NEC position and made a further collection and donation, bringing the national total to £66,342, less than five pence per member'. [4]

One such NALGO branch that showed solid support for the miners was the London Borough of Camden branch. The autumn edition of the branch magazine, *Public Eye*, led with the editorial 'Why you should support the miners' (fig 4). It went into the background of the dispute, tackled the question of whether the miners should have held a ballot before coming out on strike and went on to deal with the question of violence. 'There have been some ugly scenes. But it most cases it has been the police who have provoked the trouble with their use of truncheons, riot equipment, police horses and so on'. The editorial also pointed out that after 32 weeks of the strike two miners had died on picket lines, five were on life support

machines, three had fractured skulls, ten had broken ribs and
there were at least 2,500 cases of cracked ribs, broken arms
and torn muscles. Although the editorial reported that the
Home Office had claimed that after 32 weeks 750 police officers had been 'hurt' during the strike, there were no details
of injuries. And by the 32nd week the miners had suffered
7,100 arrests. Like many NALGO branches Camden had
set up a Miners' Support Committee and had twinned with a
coal mining community - Bentley pit in Yorkshire, working
closely with the Bentley Women's Action Group.

But it was not only miners that faced arrest. Caroline Bedale,
a NALGO steward, health & safety rep and Branch Education Secretary in the North Manchester Health branch, illustrates how local activists in her branch working with other
local trades unionists took up the call, and how she came to
be arrested.

'I was arrested on a picket line outside North Manchester
General Hospital, together with a physiotherapist from
ASTMS and a porter from NUPE. I was initially charged
with assaulting a policeman, and the physio and porter with
obstructing the highway; later the police must have decided
the assault charge was more likely to stick on a man, so they
switched it to the porter. At the magistrates' court hearing, there was a magnificent demonstration of support from
fellow health workers and miners and other trade unionists.
Our solicitors (we each had separate ones, as we were in three
different unions – I was in NALGO) did a deal, whereby the
charges were dropped if we agreed to be bound over to keep
the peace for a year. The physio and I had wanted to continue and argue our case, but the porter was facing the more
serious charge, and we all had to agree to the deal.

How had we come to this? The joint trade union committee
in North Manchester was known (even renowned) for our
militancy and organisation. Our activity had a long history,
but had been particularly galvanised by the 1982 health work-

ers' pay dispute – the first time nationally that all the health unions had acted together to try to win a better pay deal. Coinciding with the Falklands War and Thatcher's rise in popularity, our pay dispute had failed – in fact, it was at that point that the Conservative government deliberately split the nurses from other health workers by forming the Pay Review Body for them. But we had learned lessons about how to work together, and about how to gain support from other trade unions. We had held early morning pickets several times during 1982 at the local pit, Agecroft Colliery, and always got good support from the miners on our strike days and demonstrations.

So when the miners' strike started in 1984, we held meetings of members, and pledged support within our individual union branches and joint trade union committee. We made donations from our branches, we took part in all the local demonstrations, we visited the local pit picket lines and others further afield. Our arrests came on one of the TUC days of action, in the summer of 1984. As usual on such strike days, we had put a picket on the main hospital gate and were making bucket collections and asking colleagues and suppliers not to cross the picket line. Being a hospital, we always sorted out emergency cover on wards and never tried to stop ambulances with 'blue lights'. We'd never had problems with the police before (and never since), but it was clear on that day that they had instructions to treat us harshly. Right from the start they kept trying to move us away from the gate and to keep the traffic moving. The physio was a little way up the hospital drive, talking to a car driver when suddenly she was grabbed by a couple of policemen. Without thinking I rushed over to her, and began remonstrating with the police to let her go. Before I knew it, I was in an arm lock too, and being marched up the road to a waiting police van. It was only later that I found out that as she and I were being taken to the van, all hell broke loose on the picket line with fierce confrontation between the pickets and the police. Quite surprisingly only one other person was arrested!

We were all held in the local police station for a few hours, but were released in time to go to the big demonstration which was taking place in the afternoon in Manchester. Our colleagues had done us proud, contacting our branches and union regional offices and the press, and a group of them was waiting to welcome us as we were released.

Our arrests were no big deal in the light of the attacks from the police and scabs which miners themselves faced daily on their picket lines. But they were significant in that we had considered ourselves somewhat invulnerable as health workers in relation to the police. To many members who were not politically inclined, and had perhaps not been that interested in the miners' strike itself, it brought home the political nature of the strike, and the way that forces of the state would be used against anyone who sided with the miners'.

As the miners' strike continued, the arguments grew within the trade union movement about what sort of support, or indeed whether any support, should be given. The TUC failed to give a lead, and individual unions found all sorts of excuses to back away. In NALGO, the Conservative trade union group and others opposed to NALGO's national financial support for the strike forced a special conference in October, called to debate whether any more donations should be made. Speaker after speaker won massive applause arguing that we must continue our moral and financial support. But when it came to the vote, many of the delegates had clearly been mandated by their branches to vote against, as the decision was not to give any more financial support from national funds.

This reaction was unique in the trade union movement and was greeted with glee in the right-wing press. NALGO was after all the fourth largest trade union and the move was a victory for opponents of the strike and the Tory government

The move started when five NALGO branches told the
union that they intended to withhold subscriptions (collected locally) because they disagreed with the union policy
of support for the NUM. A bandwagon was rolling and other
branches passed motions of opposition to the strike and the
financial support to the NUM. A few hundred members
resigned from the union in protest at the policy, including
many police civilian staff. By August 200 branches had come
out against union policy and a special conference was called
in October.

Although the conference was a serious set-back, branches
remained free to organise support locally for miners' support
groups, but without national support from the union. 'The
ending of national financial support for the strike meant that
some branches had to scale down their official support, fear-
ful of a similar membership revolt closer to home. However,
activists everywhere continued their local support group
activities until the bitter end in March 1985'. [5]

Notes

1   Paul Mackney, *Birmingham and the Miners' Strike. A Story of Solidarity.*
Birmingham Trades Council. 1987.

2   Geoff Revell was a full-time lay member of the NUR National Executive
during the strike and one of the key figures responsible for the decisions not
to carry coal and build support for the miners in the NUR.

3   Cecil Parkinson, *Right at the Centre.* London: Weidenfeld & Nicolson.
1992, p281.

4   Mike Ironside and Roger Seifert, *Facing up to Thatcherism; The History of
Nalgo 1979 – 93.* Oxford: OUP. 2001, pp171-172.

5   ibid: p173.

The media and the miners
Granville Williams

In the aftermath of the 1984-85 strike several books were published analysing the momentous struggle, and at least one more besides *Shafted* will be published for the 25th anniversary of the strike.[1] The role of the media during the strike and afterwards remains a critical issue. Martin Adeney and John Lloyd devoted a chapter titled 'Our enemies' front line troops' in their book, published in 1986, to the way both sides used the media to present their cases. The chapter's title was taken from a piece by Nell Myers, the NUM press officer and close confidant of NUM President Arthur Scargill, which she wrote for *The Guardian* in June 1985 defending the union's hostile attitude towards the media: 'The industrial correspondents, along with broadcasting technicians, are basically our enemies' front line troops' responsible for 'a cyclone of vilification, distortion and untruth'.

Relations between the government, the NCB and the majority of the national newspapers were indeed extremely close, and the resources deployed far outweighed those that the NUM and its supporters could draw on. Nightly television news reports of violent confrontations on picket lines were powerful amplifiers of the message the government insistently promoted of, in Margaret Thatcher's repugnant phase, the miners as the 'enemy within' engaged in an anti-democratic insurrection.

The NCB was in a stronger position than the NUM in terms of communication with miners. It had the names and addresses of every miner and *Coal News*, previously only sold to miners at the pits, had its print order increased from 130,000 to 230,000 as the board took to posting it free to every miner. In the battle to persuade miners to return to work, which began in earnest from November after the failure of ACAS negotiations, a special unit was set up in Coal House, Doncaster to orchestrate the 'return to work' offensive and demoralise the striking miners. The unit worked to the NCB Chair Ian McGregor and deputy chair James Cowan and organised the national publicity offensive against the miners, whilst each coal board area also targeted local newspapers with adverts about numbers returning to work at pits in the area. The campaign began with a press statement announcing that miners who went back to work by 19 November would qualify for bonus and holiday payments which could bring their total pay packet up to £650. In the ensuing weeks a media blitz was orchestrated, with news reports using inaccurate figures, about the 'drift back to work', 'new faces' and a 'surge'. These were accompanied by a massive advertising campaign with £4.5 million spent in national and local newspapers. (figs 5 & 6) The NCB also had a well-resourced press office which paid close attention to the media, challenging what were considered to be inaccurate reports.[2]

In contrast the NUM had *The Miner*, edited by Maurice Jones, which was printed every ten days or so with a print run of 400,000 until the end of August 1984, when it was cut back to 200,000 on the grounds of cost. Nell Myers was the solitary press officer in Sheffield and if she was unavailable there was no-one else for journalists to talk to.

Peter Walker, the Energy minister, ensured that he had a comprehensive picture of media coverage. The Department of Energy paid £1,000 a week at one stage for a media monitoring agency to record any broadcast on the strike and from July 1984, onwards, when he discarded the pretence of non-involvement, the presentation of both the Coal Board's and the government's case was discussed daily. He also had easy access to newspaper editors, and their political correspondents, concentrating on the Sunday papers, especially *The News of the World* but also the *Sunday Times* and *Sunday Telegraph*. Significantly, Walker chose not to brief the industrial correspondents who were regarded as too sympathetic to the miners.

The national press in 1984, with the exception of *The Guardian*, *Daily Mirror* and *Morning Star* were slavishly pro-Thatcherite. The Tory 'wet', the late Ian Gilmour, described the role sections of it played in buttressing the anti-union, pro-privatisation agenda she pushed through: '...spurred on by a right-wing popular press which could hardly have been more fawning if it had been state-controlled - and indeed a liberal use of the honour system to knight editors and ennoble proprietors produced much the same effect - the new Thatcher government set out to solve the problems that had defied all its predecessors since 1945'.[3] The result was a stream of front-page headlines, news reports and photographs which projected an inaccurate and distorted picture of the conduct of the strike: ('Godfather Scargill's Mafia Mob', *News of the World*, 7 October 1984; 'Scargill's Real Aim Is War', *Sun*, 5 April 1984). Readers were left with a view that the strike was precipitated by the power-crazed antics of Arthur Scargill, and that the extreme measures taken by the police both at the pit gates and in the courts were caused solely by picket-line violence.

There were several flash points between print workers, angry at the blatant bias they were being asked on run on the presses, and national newspaper editors and proprietors. On 9 May 1984 the *Daily Express* carried a page one splash and centre spread in its edition devoted to a spoof speech Arthur Scargill would have made if he 'cared less about toppling a democratic government and more about the truth'. Bill Keys, the general secretary of the Society of Graphical and Allied Trades, represented some of the print workers on the paper, and demanded the right of reply to what he thought was the most politically biased article he had ever seen in his forty-seven years as a trade union official. Lord Matthews, owner of the *Daily Express*, agreed to print a reply but when Bill Keys insisted it should be on the front page the paper's editor, Sir Larry Lamb, who had written the offending piece, offered his resignation. The piece finally appeared as a 2,000 word article by Arthur Scargill on the centre pages with a picture on the paper's front page of the miners' leader at a rally in Mansfield with his arm outstretched. It was this picture which led to a dramatic confrontation between *The Sun's* editor, Kelvin MacKenzie and the paper's printers. In January 1984 MacKenzie had been challenged by the printers after he printed a 'ballot form' for miners. The printers obtained both a disclaimer and right of reply. This time when McKenzie put the bold headline 'Mine Fuhrer' with the photograph the printers refused to allow production and the paper appeared on 15 May with neither. In their place was the text: 'Members of *The Sun* production chapels refused to handle the Arthur Scargill picture and major headline of our lead story. *The Sun* has decided, reluctantly, to print the paper without either' (fig 7).

In July 1984, the fourth month of the miners' strike, Robert Maxwell acquired the *Daily Mirror* and from the start he interfered in the editorial content of the *Mirror* 'Comment' columns to reflect his views, and an article contributed by the industrial editor, Geoffrey Goodman, was altered. The most outrageous case was the Mirror headline on 10 September: 'Scargill to Ballot Members on Final Offer', a story (which he did not write) under the by-line of Terry Pattinson, and an anonymous 'Comment' entitled 'A Vote For Sanity'. The story was untrue but Maxwell printed it anyway. [4]

The cumulative impact of the propaganda assault on the miners by the overwhelming majority of the national newspapers was to present to their readers over several months a totally distorted view of the strike.

The performance of the broadcast media during the strike also came in for severe criticism, especially because both the Independent Broadcasting Authority, which regulated commercial broadcasting, and the BBC were required to be impartial in their coverage of industrial issues. But in fact coverage on the main news channels of the central issues of the dispute (the ballot, violence, the return to work movement, the personality of Arthur Scargill and 'uneconomic' pits) was framed in terms which favoured the NCB and the government. The issues the miners were fighting for (keeping pits open, defending jobs and communities) were marginalised or dismissed, with the exception of Channel 4 News which did attempt to explore issues and allow the NUM space to present its point of view. Channel 4 also broadcast a series of documentaries which were sympathetic to the striking miners and their communities - the *People to People* programmes and Coal Not Dole, for example. ITV was not happy with Ken Loach's *Which Side Are You On?* commissioned by Melvyn Bragg for the South Bank Show in November 1984. The programme, an anthology of songs and poems inspired by the strike, particularly the role of the police and the media in the dispute, was considered too biased to be broadcast. It was shown instead on Channel 4 in January 1985 but the IBA required a 'balancing' programme to go out with it – Jimmy Reid criticising Arthur Scargill in a Comment piece.

The impact of biased or non-existent coverage of the real experiences of tens of thousands of people in mining communities is captured well by David Thacker, a television and theatre director, describing the content of the interviews he tape-recorded in Barnburgh, near Doncaster after the strike:

'Running through all the accounts we heard were two central themes. Firstly, there was the appalling violence and brutality of the police during the strike. Both in the small scale of their everyday activities, and their major operations to occupy whole communities – they were like a foreign invader occupying entire villages and towns...

They were outraged that no-one knew about these things. This was the second recurring theme. They were astonished by the wall of silence in the media. Their experiences were never reflected nor reported on the TV. The violence they experienced and the occupation of their villages was never mentioned. On the contrary there was enormous media distortion of the facts. Even the papers that were supposed to support them, like the *Daily Mirror*, talked about the violence of the pickets but kept quiet about the brutality of the so-called forces of law and order.'[5]

The other criticism by miners was the reduction of the strike to a conflict between powerful personalities. As one miner commented:

'Even before the strike, I did not have a very high regard for the media, especially the tabloids; in particular, the *Sun*, the *Daily Star*, the *Daily Mail* and the *Express*, there isn't a good one amongst them. I object to the way they have personalised the strike as if it's between Arthur Scargill and MacGregor because that ignores all of us on strike and our views, along with the issues that we are striking for which are beginning to get lost'.[6]

Martin Adeney and John Lloyd concluded their chapter on the role of the media:

'...press and media relations were not a sideshow. They were one of the central battlegrounds, and the continued failure of NUM leaders to swing public opinion, including that of their own members, decisively to their side, in spite of the self-inflicted wounds of the Coal Board, was a key factor in their defeat.'[7]

The Campaign for Press and Broadcasting Freedom (CPBF) saw it differently in 1985 when it published *Media Hits The Pits*:

'No one could realistically claim that the media played the decisive role in the outcome of the coal dispute. But it undoubtedly played an important role in consistently reinforcing the Government/NCB, and systematically undermining and demoralising striking miners and their supporters. However it has also generated considerable unease at the role of the media and revealed more widespread criticism of its inadequacies. In particular it has unleashed a powerful dynamic for the right of reply...' [8]

The key point is that with or without media support a cause can be won or lost but the political climate in 1984-85 was unremittingly hostile to trades unionism. During the Falklands War the government openly managed the news.[9] On the back of the Argentinian defeat Thatcher won re-election and then fought the miners with the same tenacity as she conducted the Falklands campaign. Unfortunately the Labour and trade union movement, with important exceptions, did not mobilise to fight back and support the miners with a corresponding tenacity.

Opposing voices and images

The CPBF did not, however, sit on the sidelines. We worked tirelessly to build links between media workers and the NUM and energetically to promote the right of reply. Media coverage became a big issue and in this we were prominent. Television news and current affairs programmes featured the organisation, as did radio phone-ins, and letters and articles appeared in a wide range of printed media. We were part of a much broader solidarity movement which used a diverse range of media to support the miners' cause. Fleet Street workers, who raised £2 million during the strike, also produced two *Right of Reply* specials which sold widely and raised thousands of pounds for the miners. *The Miners' Campaign Tapes* were produced for the NUM by ten of the film and video workshops accredited by ACTT and widely distributed. *Leeds Postcards Miners' Strike Account* raised over £30,000 from donations and the sale of a set of eight postcards incorporating a design by Paul Morton (fig 8). Sales of a stunning collection of photographs, *Blood Sweat &Tears*, taken by photographers from an explicit perspective of support for the miners raised over £6,000 from sales towards the NUM hardship fund for victimised miners. All the royalties from *Deep Digs! Cartoons of the Miners' Strike* (fig 9) went to Women Against Pit Closures. [11]

And of course there was the music, both during and after the strike, in support of the miners, either at benefit concerts or through the songs and records of a diverse range of musicians: the folk songs of Dick Gaughan, Shoulder to Shoulder which drew together Test Dept and the South Wales Striking Miners Choir, The Redskins, The Mekons, Chumbawamba, Billy Bragg, and many more (fig 10).

There was also an outpouring of creative expression from miners and their families about the impact of the powerful, life-changing struggle they were involved in. Sam Palfrey has a good survey of the range of writing produced, and in particular the humour generated in adversity.[12] In a book like this it is difficult to capture this very important aspect of mining life but one example, among many, is the story of the snowman on the picket line. The incident, depending on the writer (see below page 54), happened at various collieries: Bold, Silverwood, Cortonwood, and so on. Dave Douglass tells it like this in *All Power To The Imagination:*

'The miners of Silverwood, having been told they were confined to six pickets only, built themselves a seventh comrade in the shape of a large snowman, wearing for good measure a plastic policeman's helmet.

Next morning, Chief Inspector Nesbitt appears on the scene and seeing the jeering miners and their steely eyed companion, ordered the constables to knock it down. This order brought rebellion to the police ranks as PCs declined to, "look so fucking stupid knocking down a snowman". "Very well," shouts the irate Nesbitt, jumping in his Range Rover and charging off to demolish the snowman, as pickets ran laughing for cover.

Maybe it was a trick of the light, or maybe a twinkle glistened in the icy countenance on the snowman's fixed expression - we shall never know, as the Range Rover made contact and came to a dead stop, smashing front grill, bumper and headlamps and hurling the shocked Nesbitt into the steering wheel. PCs found excuses to walk away or suppress body-shaking laughter while pickets fell about on the ground with side splitting mirth. The snowman had been constructed around a three foot high two foot thick concrete post!'

My own limited, and fallible, research suggests that the incident did happen at Brentwood Colliery in Yorkshire. The first snowman, with toy policeman's helmet, was just that and the inspector kicked it down so the miners built the second one around the concrete bollard and the enraged inspector drove his vehicle at it.

Small independent presses such as Yorkshire Art Circus and Bannerworks of Huddersfield published a steady stream of books. Canary Press published *Hearts and Minds* and *Shifting Horizons* both dealing with the activities of women in the Nottinghamshire mining communities as well as *State of Siege: Politics and Policing in the Miners' Strike* and *A Turn of the Screw*, which dealt with the fate of the hundreds of sacked, victimised and imprisoned miners.

The miners' strike and the closure of Ledston Luck in 1986 gave Harry Malkin the opportunity to shape another way of life, developing the skills to record, in a powerful series of paintings, 'the trials, tribulations and conditions' of coal mining (fig 11). Amber Films in the North East produced a trilogy of films, *The Scar* (1997), *Like Father* (2001) and *Shooting Magpies* (2005), set in the former East Durham pit villages which tackled unflinchingly the human dimensions behind the collapse of the mining economy and culture.

Two very different books published on the 10th anniversary by young miners active in the strike deserve mention. *Miners: 1984-1994*, edited with a combative introduction by Joe Owens, collects together the personal stories of Scottish miners and the effect on their lives of the strike and its aftermath.[13] Richard Clarkson, now sadly no longer alive, recorded his year on strike at the Prince of Wales pit, Pontefract, in *Striking Memories*. He created, like Ken Wilkinson from Askern Colliery near Doncaster, a photographic record of the strike. Richard's photos, along with other badges, leaflets and items collected during the strike, were in *Striking Images*, an exhibition at the Elizabethan Gallery, Wakefield between May-July 1994. Ken Wilkinson's photos were exhibited at the National Coal Mining Museum for England in November 2008 (figs 12 & 13). He comments, 'It is hard to believe that in such a short time my life as a miner and those of many others, along with many mining communities, are now considered history' [14]

Once the economic foundations supporting mining communities were knocked from under them the consequences of the disintegration, pain and dislocation of mining communities rarely featured in the London-based national media. It fell to the local, often weekly, newspapers to report the human dimensions of the calamity which miners and their families confronted.

Notes

1   Martin Adeney and John Lloyd, *The Miners' Strike 1984-85: Loss Without Limit*. London: Routledge. 1986; Alex Callinicos and Mike Simons, *The Great Strike: The miners' strike 1984-85 and its lessons*. London: Socialist Worker. 1985; Geoffrey Goodman, *The Miners' Strike*. London: Pluto Press. 1985; Nicholas Jones, *Strikes and the Media*. Oxford: Blackwell. 1986; Sunday Times Insight Team, *Strike*. London: Andre Deutsch. 1985. *Marching to the Fault Line: The Miners' Strike 1984-85* by Francis Beckett

and David Hencke was also published for the 25th anniversary.

2   Jones, 1986, pp 98-99.

3   Ian Gilmour, *Dancing With Dogma: Britain Under Thatcherism*. London: Simon and Schuster. 1992, p2

4   Tom Bower, *Maxwell: The Outsider*. London: William Heinemann. 1991, pp 384-388.

5   David Thacker used the mining community interviews for the Old Vic production *The Enemies Within*. He also directed *Faith*, a drama about the miners' strike broadcast on BBC1 in February 2005. Phil Mitchinson's interview with him is at: *http://www.marxist.com/britain-interview-david-thacker010505.htm*

6   Jim Coulter, Susan Miller & Martin Walker, *A State of Siege. Politics and Policing of the Coalfields: Miners' Strike 1984*. London: Canary Press. 1984, p190.

7   Adeney and Lloyd, p 256.

8   David Jones, Julian Petley, Mike Power, Lesley Wood, *Media Hits The Pits*. London: CPBF. 1985.

9   Robert Harris, *Gotcha! The Media, the Government and the Falklands Crisis*. London: Faber & Faber. 1983

10   Roger Huddle, Angela Phillips, Mike Simons and John Sturrock, *Blood Sweat & Tears: Photographs From The Great Miners' Strike 1984-85*. London: Artworker Books. 1985.

11   *Deep Digs! Cartoons of the Miners' Strike*. London: Pluto Press. 1985.

12   Sammy Palfrey *Writing and the Miners' Strike 1984-85* from Working Class Museum and Library, Salford, Bulletin 12. Available at: *http://www.wcml.org.uk/culture/miners.htm*

13   Joe Owens, *Miners 1984-1994: A Decade of Endurance*. Edinburgh: Polygon. 1994

14   Richard Clarkson's collection of 135 photos are online at *http://www.wakefieldmuseumcollections.org.uk*

Covering Coal in Yorkshire
Peter Lazenby

I have been a newspaper reporter for 41 years, working from 1967 to 1972 on a weekly paper in Otley, in the Wharfe Valley in Yorkshire, and from 1972 up to the present on the *Yorkshire Evening Post* in Leeds.

The *Yorkshire Evening Post* is part of the Yorkshire Post Newspapers group. Up to 1969 the company title was Yorkshire Conservative Newspapers; then the name was changed. On starting work there I was informed at an induction meeting that 'only the name has changed'.

I became the paper's Industrial Reporter in 1974, a key job at a time when Yorkshire was an industrial powerhouse employing hundreds of thousands of people in the coal mining, steel, textile and tailoring industries.

I covered the successful miners' strike of 1974, and the Lofthouse colliery disaster, bringing me into contact with close-knit Yorkshire pit communities for the first time.

Most establishment newspapers had an in-built bias against trades unions in general, and the miners and their union, the NUM, in particular. For example, as Industrial Reporter of the *Yorkshire Evening Post* I was expected to contact the then National Coal Board (NCB) every New Year's Day to be told how many miners had 'blobbed' work that day (New Year's Day was not then a Bank Holiday). This was deemed newsworthy, and was used to attack the miners, complete with leader (opinion) column comments about their 'fecklessness' and 'irresponsibility.' The leader writers applied no such criticism to directors and chief executives who chose to clear their New Year hangovers with a game of golf.

In 1973 Arthur Scargill became President of Yorkshire

area of the NUM, covering the biggest coalfield in Britain, before he became national union President eight years later. The union's Yorkshire Area Council met monthly, and Arthur Scargill staged a Press conference after each Council meeting. One of the Yorkshire coalfield's 65-or-so pits was Sharlston, outside Wakefield. The union secretary there was Charlie Churm, in NUM terms a right-winger with no time for Arthur Scargill. Some reporters as a matter of course contacted him after each Area Council meeting, often giving prominence to his verbal attacks on Arthur Scargill, rather than factual reports of the decisions of the Area Council. These would be used as a main plank of the subsequent story. Charlie Churm used to burn his pit's allocation of the radical *Yorkshire Miner* newspaper in his garden, to prevent it from being read by his members.

When in 1981 Arthur Scargill stood for the position of national President as Joe Gormley approached retirement, there was one candidate from the union's right against him, Trevor Bell. Unlike Arthur Scargill, who had been an underground worker on the coal face, Trevor Bell was an office worker, an official of the NUM's white-collar office staff section COSA. When stories about the election appeared in the Yorkshire Evening Post a senior sub regularly called for a photo of Trevor Bell to be used 'in his pit gear'. Trevor Bell did not work underground. He went there only occasionally. The aim of using a photo of him with pit gear on – miner's helmet, lamp and so on – was clear. It was a futile attempt to persuade real miners to identify with him and vote for him, and against Arthur Scargill, in the election. This was another small example of the day-to-day manipulation of the news. In fact Arthur Scargill won the election by the biggest majority in the NUM's history.

By the strike of 1984 Charlie Churm had gone, and when the strike began the miners of Sharlston came out.

The strike saw most of the newspaper industry swing into

action against the miners. In Leeds it was no different.

At the *Yorkshire Evening Post*, NCB statements were daily accepted as fact. There was little effort to ensure balance by giving the NUM an opportunity to respond. That only happened if individual reporters took it upon themselves to contact union representatives. NCB statements were often going direct to sub-editors through the national news agency the Press Association with little or no involvement of reporters on the papers receiving them.

Placid acceptance of NCB claims was a feature during the NCB's 'back to work' campaign. With the police preventing most of the pits of Nottinghamshire and the Midlands from being effectively picketed, the NCB turned its attention to those areas which were, in the main, rock solid, like Yorkshire.

As the strike continued into the autumn and winter of 1984, a slow trickle of miners began to return to work, forced to do so by hardship and the suffering of their families. The NCB Press office issued daily figures giving the number of miners who had supposedly decided to break the strike and return to work. The numbers were listed pit by pit. These were accepted as fact. The gist of the stories was that the trickle back to work was becoming a flood. I saw no evidence of any efforts to check the NCB figures with other sources, especially the NUM.

The NCB would make great play of a pit 'resuming production', announcing that coal had been 'turned' at such-and-such a pit. Again, this appeared to be accepted as fact by the media.

I contacted the NUM at some individual pits where production was reported by the NCB to have resumed, and was told that the number of men working was so small that it would have been physically impossible to have resumed production. What the NCB termed a resumption of production was a mystery to them.

The daily drip drip of 'back to work' figures was intended to persuade more striking miners that the strike was lost, and to encourage them to return to work. The press dutifully played its part in promoting the propaganda.

Then there was the mystical figure of 'Silver Birch'.

Silver Birch was a miner whose name was Chris Butcher. He travelled around striking coalfields taking part in 'back to work' meetings. The Press built him up into a clandestine hero akin to the fictional Scarlet Pimpernel.

Similarly the breakaway strike-breaking group which became the Union of Democratic Mineworkers was given heroic status by the press.

The press regionally and nationally parroted unquestioningly the oft-repeated lie that 'there is no pit closures programme'. The enormity of the lie was to be illustrated by events which followed the strike.

One incident was typical of the approach taken by sections of the media. When the young striking miner David Jones was killed in a picket line incident, the NUM told me that one national tabloid daily paper despatched a reporter and photographer to his parents' home in the hope of persuading them to blame the union, the strike, and Arthur Scargill for their son's death. They refused.

There was also a continual focus on alleged 'picket line violence'. The assumption – and according to much of the media, a statement of fact - was that strikers caused the violence, despite evidence showing that police, who had been mobilised against the miners as a national force, used violence against pickets, in some instances invading Yorkshire mining communities en masse.

There was the infamous action, admitted years later, when BBC TV changed the sequence of events filmed at Orgreave, the coking plant near Rotherham in South Yorkshire. The BBC showed pickets attacking police with whatever missiles were at hand – stones, bricks, wooden staves, branches –

followed by a police cavalry charge in retaliation. The truth was that mounted police launched a baton-wielding charge against the picketing miners, injuring dozens. The miners then retaliated. It was not until the 1990s that the BBC admitted it had reversed the sequence of events.

Having said all that, looking back through my cuttings of the period, the *Yorkshire Evening Post* did publish a number of stories showing striking miners in a more positive light. My recollection is that these stories appeared despite the system, not because of it. I like to assume that on regional newspapers in coal mining areas across Britain, newspaper reporters, members of the National Union of Journalists, were doing what they could to achieve a degree of balance over coverage of the strike.

In our case for example there was the story of Charlie Livingstone, the ex-paratrooper who was a miner at Sharlston. He was also a singer-guitarist, and recorded his own song 'Get Off Your Knees' to raise funds for miners' families. I still have a copy of the record.

There was the former Coldstream Guardsman Gordon Jones, a miner at South Kirkby colliery. He sent the medal awarded to him for service in Northern Ireland back to the Queen in protest at the Government's pit closure plans (plans which, according to the NCB and the Government, did not exist). We carried that story.

There was Lorna Cohen, the Leeds Labour Councillor who launched a fund to pay for the funeral of a 14 years old boy from Upton, near Wakefield, who died picking coal from a spoil heap. His family had been refused state benefits because his miner father was on strike. They could not afford the funeral fees.

There were stories of hardship, and of resilience in the pit communities, where food kitchens were established in the same way they had been set up in the miners' strike of 1926.

There were other media bright spots.

On one occasion the NCB released to the press, including the *Yorkshire Evening Post*, a batch of letters said to be written by miners opposed to the strike and calling for it to end. The *Yorkshire Evening Post* intended to publish a page of them, with no response from the NUM or from striking miners.

I was approached by two printers who were lay officers of the printers' union the National Graphical Association (NGA) at the *Yorkshire Evening Post*. The printers were extremely unhappy about the instruction to publish the anti-strike letters with no balancing contribution from miners supporting the strike.

We discussed how printers on *The Sun* had refused to use a doctored picture of Arthur Scargill, with one arm raised, making him appear to be making a Nazi salute. In fact he had both arms raised acknowledging applause at a rally when the photo was taken. I was there. *The Sun* simply 'cropped' one arm off to get the desired effect. As a result of the printers' refusal to use the doctored picture *The Sun* had white space instead of the photo.

Half an hour after our conversation I was approached by my editor. He informed me that the NGA had decided to 'take over editorship of the paper' - that the NGA reps had said there would be no paper the next day unless the NCB letters were balanced by publication of letters putting an alternative view from miners supporting the strike. I was asked if I could get hold of such letters from the NUM.

I drove from Leeds to Sheffield to the home of Maurice Jones, editor of the NUM newspaper *The Miner*, who had sacks full of letters from miners supporting the strike. A selection was published the next day alongside those issued by the NCB.

The *Yorkshire Evening Post* NGA's act of solidarity was recognised with a letter of thanks to them from Arthur Scargill. That was the only recognition they wanted.

There were other lighter, positive events during the strike, some of which received publicity.

Kellingley colliery at Knottingley in West Yorkshire was Britain's first 'super pit' producing more than 1m tonnes of coal a year. At its peak the pit employed 3,000 miners.

In the 1970s and early 1980s the NUM branch secretary there was Jimmy Miller, a Scot, a Communist Party member, and a gifted orator.

Jimmy retired shortly before the strike and returned to his native Scotland. His son Davey, another fine speaker, was elected to the job of branch secretary against four other candidates.

Davey gained fame, and media publicity, during the strike for two actions. He carried an organ donor card, and on it he wrote the words 'not for use by any Tory over the age of 16'. The card was turned into a postcard by Leeds Postcards, a co-operative which produced many such 'alternative' cards for causes on the left. Davey Miller's organ donor postcard was sold to raise money for the strike.

Davey also made a speech in which he said: 'The miners will eat grass before they will go back to work,' a quote which was repeated by him in the press and on one other notable occasion.

Every day hundreds of striking miners would gather at Kellingley to leave for picketing duties in Nottinghamshire and elsewhere at pits which had not joined the strike. They were given breakfast in the 'Big K', the miners' social centre built with miners' money under the leadership of Jimmy Miller. When they returned each evening, sometimes bloodied and battered, they were given an evening meal.

It was plain fare as resources were of course scarce. By winter of 1984 the pickets must have been sick of the sight of baked beans.

But on one occasion, which as far as I know went unreported, an ageing Volvo estate car pulled into the car park of the Big K. It was driven by Jimmy Miller from Scotland. In the back was a whole stag.

Nobody asked Jimmy where it had come from. A local butcher was called in to deal with the beast, the social club kitchen went into overdrive, and it was roasted and served to the pickets when they returned that night.

As they sat down to the meal Davey Miller stood up, and recalled the speech in which he had said the miners would eat grass before they would return to work.

And then he added the words: 'And if there's no grass they'll eat venison.'

There was the tale, probably apocryphal, of the miners who built a snowman on their picket line in the winter of 1984, decorating it with a plastic policeman's helmet. A police inspector reportedly kicked it to pieces. By the next morning it had been re-built. This time the inspector drove a police vehicle at the offending snowman. However the pickets had built it around a concrete bollard. I was told the incident happened at Peckfield colliery, outside Leeds. It was probably reported as having happened at any number of pits.

I believe I hold the dubious honour of being the first journalist to be arrested on duty during the strike, though I'll stand to be corrected if anyone else can make the claim.

The police were operating a legally questionable policy of restricting the movement of miners trying to picket working pits. This was being challenged by lawyers. I travelled with a group of pickets from Yorkshire to Nottinghamshire to see at first hand what the police were doing.

There were three miners and myself in a car being driven by one of the pickets. We set off from Barnsley and headed for Nottinghamshire. We turned off the motorway and neared the target pit. A police patrol car drove up behind us and told us to stop.

The miners were open about who they were and what they were planning to do - join a picket already manned by their Nottinghamshire colleagues and persuade other miners to join the strike. The police told them they must leave Nottinghamshire. They would be escorted to the county boundary, and if they returned they would be arrested.

After escorting us to the boundary the police car drove off. Our driver took the next turning off the motorway and headed back towards the pit. The car was stopped again by police. One radio call was made by police, revealing that the car had already been stopped once and escorted out of the county. The police told us we were under arrest.

The driver was removed from the car and taken away. The remaining three of us were told we were being cautioned and released, and we were again told to leave the county. Another of the miners drove, again under police escort. This time we didn't return.

The *Yorkshire Evening Post* ran the story of the arrest, and the limitations on freedom of movement being imposed on miners, on its front page the next day, under the headline 'Nabbed!' To his credit one director of the paper called for legal action against the police on my behalf for wrongful arrest. He was dissuaded by colleagues.

As far as I recall Paul Routledge, labour editor of *The Times*, was next to be arrested while carrying out a similar assignment.

Journalists were not exempt from the attentions of the more secretive forces of the state. My home telephone was tapped. On more than one occasion my 'phone would ring, and on answering it I would hear a recording of a telephone conversation I had just had. Many others I have spoken to had the same experience.

Closures

Decimated is a word often used incorrectly, but in the case of the scale of the destruction of the coal mining industry after the miners' strike of 1984-85 it is an understatement. The final destruction in the early 1990s also saw a sea change in the attitude of some sections of the media towards the miners. Indeed in Yorkshire there was outspoken sympathy and support for the pit communities.

It is important to understand the scale of the devastation. In 1983 there were around 200,000 miners working at some 200 pits in Britain. The Yorkshire coalfield represented between one quarter and one third of them, around 60,000 miners at 60 pits. The Yorkshire coalfield was so huge that for administrative purposes the NCB broke it up into four areas – South Yorkshire, Doncaster, Barnsley and North Yorkshire. North Yorkshire was a geographic misnomer, as it covered pits in the Wakefield, Castleford, Leeds and Pontefract districts of West Yorkshire. It also took in the Selby coalfield complex of five pits, created at a cost of £1b in taxpayers' money.

Today there are less than 4,000 deep coal miners in Britain, and a handful of pits. In my part of the world, West and North Yorkshire, only one pit remains, Kellingley at Knottingley, near Pontefract. It was the first in Europe to produce 1m tonnes of coal a year, and at its peak it employed 3,000 miners. Today around 400 miners produce 2m tonnes of coal a year at Kellingley.

With the strike over, the closures accelerated, culminating in the final butchery of most of the remaining pits by the Conservatives in the early 1990s. They were privatised for a pittance. Arthur Scargill's predictions of widespread closures, derided by the media during the strike, proved to be an underestimate.

Significantly, after the strike one of the first NCB operations to be shut was the industry's advanced coal technology research plant at Grimethorpe, in South Yorkshire. The plant carried with it the future of coal in Britain. Its technicians were seeking ways to burn coal more cleanly, without the destructive environmental side-effects caused by carbon and sulphur. The closure was an indication of the Conservative Government's plans for the future of the industry – a future which was bleak indeed.

The steady abandonment of the industry, and of an estimated 200 years of coal reserves, also brought warnings about Britain's future energy resources. During the strike North Sea gas was burned in vast quantities to create electricity at hastily built gas-fuelled power stations. This continued after the strike. The Government was told that if the North Sea stocks were reserved for domestic use – homes, hospitals etc, rather than for making electricity – then they might last as long as two centuries. The government was also told that burning the gas in the huge quantities needed to generate electricity meant they would run out in 20 to 30 years' time, leaving Britain dependent on gas supplies from unstable regions including parts of Eastern Europe and the Middle East. That is what happened.

Aside from the effects on Britain's energy supplies, the closures also meant disaster for the communities which provided the pits' workforces. In most cases the pit was the sole economic base of the community. Today, despite investment in projects intended to cushion the blow brought by closure, many former pit communities are still struggling to deal with the effects of the disaster.

Sharlston colliery outside Wakefield had a healthy future. A new seam had been opened at a cost of £12m. At its peak it employed 2,200 men and produced 1m tonnes of coal a year.

The pit had been the heart of the economy of Sharlston since it was sunk in 1873 - more than a century of coal production. The village of New Sharlston which had grown up around the pit, and the population which occupied it, were there for one purpose according to the local NUM: to provide workers for the pit. Generation after generation of Sharlston teenagers followed their fathers and grandfathers down the pit.

The pit fell victim to the Tories' closure programme of

the early 1900s. By 1993 the pithead was derelict, the shaft sealed, and the community destroyed - one of the final 30-plus pits targeted by the Conservatives for destruction, an act of unforgivable venom.

Sixteen years on and the 60 hectare colliery site at Sharlston is to be 'de-contaminated,' and used for housing, heathland, agriculture, woodland and wetland. It will also be the site for an opencast mine – a quarry – to recover 400,000 tonnes of coal, 100,000 tonnes of fireclay and 377,000 tonnes of red shale.

The project will not however replace the jobs of the 2,000-plus miners who worked there.

Nor can the loss of a pit be seen in purely economic terms. Thanks mainly to the NUM, the pit brought discipline to the mining communities. One man's life depended on the man working next to him. There was comradeship, brotherhood. The young men of the community were introduced to that discipline and responsibility.

The union branch was of enormous importance in the daily lives of the miners and their branches. At Kellingley colliery the union used the co-operative buying power of 3,000 miners and their families to buy consumer goods at huge discounts. If a Kellingley miner wanted a new TV, or a washer, or a set of car tyres, he went to the union co-operative run by the branch officials. Miners paid a small weekly sum to the union over and above their subscriptions so that when a purchase was made the family did not face a big bill. It was paid gradually. The Kellingley co-operative operation was so large that the union branch had its own warehouse at the pithead. Later the warehouse was shut by the management during a dispute at the pit. This was reported in the *Yorkshire Evening Post*.

The miners' social club at Kellingley was built on the same co-operative basis, with miners making small weekly donations. The club was an ambitious project, even for a pit the size of Kellingley, and even for a man of the abilities of NUM branch secretary Jimmy Miller, who was the inspiration behind it. He wanted miners to have access to education, books, to quality entertainment, sporting and leisure facilities. He saw no reason why miners and their families should not visit a good restaurant on a Saturday night and enjoy steak and a decent bottle of wine. This was in the 1960s and 1970s, when such ambition for working class people was seen elsewhere as preposterous. Not by Jimmy Miller though. The Big K social club which the miners' money built included a fine restaurant, and all the facilities he had wanted.

The club is still there. Most of the men and their families who used it are gone.

Not only miners were affected by the closures. It was estimated that for every miner's job seven more existed in ancillary industries – engineers and technicians who made some of the most advanced mining equipment in the world, transport workers on road and rail, retail staff and many more. All these too were sacrificed.

The final stages of the closures in the early 1990s brought a wave of public support. Much of the media represented the public mood. *The Yorkshire Evening Post* published a special supplement, which I edited, in support of the miners' case. It included a series of images of a miner's lamp burning brightly, then gradually dimming to black. But media support and sympathy came too late. The media in general, and the press in particular, had played their role in the destruction of a workforce and an industry whose like will probably never be seen again in Britain.

It wasn't all about Arthur:
alternative media and the miners' strike.
Tony Harcup

There were some striking photographs published during the 1984-5 dispute, but this wasn't one of them. It had no people in, for a start, just cardboard boxes containing assorted tins of beans, tomatoes, corned beef and the like. At the top was one on which someone – judging by the writing, probably me - had written in giant felt tip pen: 'Food for miners – donate in this box.' It also sported a glued-on masthead from the weekly alternative newspaper in whose scruffy city centre office the box had been filled by contributors and readers alike: *Leeds Other Paper,* or *LOP* to its friends. The picture was published in the 15 June 1984 issue of the paper, captioned: 'Food collected in Leeds at Kellingley strike HQ. (Your LOP photographer freely admits he fiddled the arrangement of boxes so one was prominent!)'

It was a bit amateurish and more than a bit anarchic, which was pretty much the spirit of the alternative local papers that flowered across the UK from the late 1960s to the mid 1980s. Such alternative media did not pretend to be disinterested bystanders or objective observers of the miners' strike (fig 14). *LOP* was openly on the side of the strikers.

That did not mean peddling lies; we always felt the truth was on our side. Nor did it mean lecturing the National Union of Mineworkers on tactics; there was more than enough hectoring to be found in papers produced by assorted left-wing parties. Instead, it meant reporting from the miners' side of the picket lines and beyond. It also meant doing something about it by becoming part of the collective effort by trade unionists and other supporters to offer practical help.

So the alternative local press became more than a means

by which readers could find out what was happening in the coalfield communities, it offered a way for observers to become actors. When *LOP* launched a column for striking miners to appeal for the donation of larger items, the first Wanted notice read: 'For family in Pontefract: pram, cot, nappies, babyclothes for baby expected in early July.' I wonder if that strike baby, who would be 25 years old in the summer of 2009, knows of the community self-help that helped nurture him or her.

An ethos of self-organisation

Such mutual aid was a side of the strike that rarely featured in mainstream media at the time, most of which seemed obsessed with the personality of Arthur Scargill or repeating loaded phrases such as 'uneconomic pits', 'picket line violence', and later the 'drift back to work'. But it was a side of the strike that appealed particularly to those involved in alternative media, because such media themselves sprang out of a similar ethos of self-organisation: if you don't like something, get off your arse and do something about it. And if you don't know how, find out; just as groups of untrained and unpaid people had taught themselves how to become alternative journalists.

The beginning of the miners' strike happened to coincide with one of that era's occasional national conferences of alternative papers. Not content with just talking about things, those at the weekend gathering also managed to produce the *Other Voice*, described as 'a one-off national alternative newspaper composed of articles taken from recent issues of various local papers'. The front-page splash featured claims that members of the British army parachute regiment were secretly being used to bolster police ranks confronting miners' picket lines. That the story came from the *Brighton Voice* was an indication of the way in which the miners' strike impacted upon members of an alternative public sphere even in areas far from the coalfields. By reporting on the network of regional activists, and by covering the visits of striking miners and members of the nascent coalfield women's support groups who toured the country spreading their message, a national struggle could become a local story. The *Other Voice* also featured a detailed double page analysis of the economics of the energy industry, contributed by exactly the type of expert favoured in alternative media: Ken Capstick, a striking miner and NUM activist.

'Small need not mean insignificant'

Taking part in that April 1984 conference in Leeds were representatives of *Brighton Voice*, *Bush News* (London), *Coventry News*, *Durham Street Press*, *Greenwaves*, *Hull Post*, *Islington Gutter Press*, *Leeds Other Paper*, *Nottingham City Wise*, *The Other Paper* (Burton-on-Trent), *Sheep Worrying*, *Sheffield City Issues*, *Spen Valley Spark*, and *York Free Press*. They wrote the following statement about what they were up to:

'An unambiguous definition of an 'alternative newspaper' is impossible, but there seem to be features common to all of them. They are: local; anti-racist; anti-sexist; politically on the left; overtly, rather than covertly, political; not produced for profit; editorially free of the influence of advertisers; run on broadly collective principles. The content and format of individual publications is often determined by their perception of their role as persuasive or informative, by their aims and distribution, and the political allegiance of their contributors.

The precise emphasis of a paper will be dependent upon the geographical location and political arena in which it is produced. While some papers, generally in Conservative controlled areas, can count upon the wide support of the left, others in traditional Labour areas are not guaranteed such support. Thus, their role as critics of the local state will differ. A Labour establishment can be as hostile as a Tory one to the independent critical voice of the alternative newspaper.

Papers in Labour controlled areas have a contradictory role in that they often want to criticise from the left, do not want to be identified directly with the Labour party, but at the same time are loath to provide the right with ammunition.

Most alternative newspapers are small, their existence precarious. With one or two notable exceptions their circulations are in the hundreds rather than the thousands. But this tells us nothing about their influence nor their value. As virtually all the mass media are in the political centre or on the right, the voice of the local alternative newspaper is an important counterweight. Small need not mean insignificant.'

Diverse as they were, such papers formed only part of the alternative media. There were groups who used film or video rather than print to provide an alternative to what the mainstream had to offer, and there were also national publications such as the feminist magazine *Spare Rib*, community newspapers, fanzines such as *Wake Up* (which released a miners' benefit record featuring Billy Bragg and the Redskins), and numerous pamphlets, leaflets, posters, songs, artwork, postcards, stickers, badges, even graffiti – all of which could be considered as forms of alternative media.

'It was their struggle rather than Scargill's'

One of those who helped draft the 1984 conference statement was *LOP*'s Gordon Wilson. Interviewed a decade later,[1] he described how alternative media approached the dispute:

'The miners' strike was a good example of us giving a commitment to a struggle. There was some food going out to Knottingley and they asked us to send someone to take a photograph on the Friday night. I went and was

Figure 1 Syd Bailey at the former site of Cortonwood Colliery
Photograph Andy Boag

»

Sid Bailey

Cortonwood Colliery

When I first came to Cortonwood in 1958 there was about eight hundred men, by the time the strike came along there was about five or six hundred. I worked at Cortonwood for 28 years. I came to Cortonwood for reconstruction, development. When the pit closed I was still an underground worker working on developments. 25 years ago there was none of this infrastructure you see here today, it was a colliery. The baths were roughly where we looked at Morrison's, at the end of the car park. I was on the day shift when news came underground that the pit was closing in a fortnight. It was a big shock for everybody; I thought the pit would have gone on quite some time after that. The powers that be felt it was the right pit to shut at that time, and then we learned there was going to be more pits shut of course, and there were. It was said there was going to be twenty pits, but there were far more than twenty pits in the country that closed at the finish. It was very sad; I was expecting to stop in mining until I retired.

I didn't expect the pits to close; it's not a thing that I thought about. We knew we had got to move on, we knew we had to earn a living, and that's what we did. We got some redundancy money, but that soon went when you're not getting a wage in. Some of the older men found it a bit difficult, because let's face it, people didn't want older men without any specific skills.

People had worked in the pit all their lives and that was their trade and they were great at that job, but they didn't really know any other trade so it was difficult for a lot of people.

During the strike we weren't getting paid anything, it was very difficult for twelve months. You couldn't pay your rent, you couldn't pay anything, and bills were going up. When you got back to work you were paying double everything to catch up; double rent, double stamps, the national insurance that you'd missed, it was double everything coming out of your wages. It was very difficult.

In the pit you built up some very good friends. Your safety depended on everybody else. If you saw anybody in difficulty, everybody took time to help out. It was fantastic, I enjoyed working in the pit, but when we came out, it was a different world and you just had to adapt, and there was no two ways about it.

Figure 2 'The State Funeral' © Dave Brown 2008. First published in *The Independent*, 14 July 2008

Figure 3 Hackney Miners' Support group leaflet and **Figure 4** front cover of Camden NALGO branch newsletter *Public Eye* (Photo Raissa Page) Children wear T-shirts for the Bentley Women's Action Group's 'Sponsor a child for Christmas' appeal.

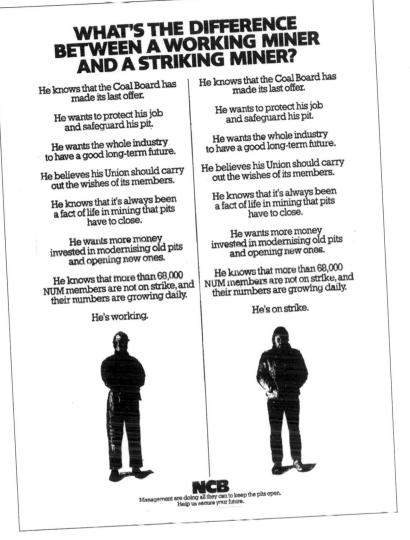

Figure 5 An example of NCB's advertising campaign. This one appeared in the *Sunday Express*, 2 December 1984

National Coal Board,
NORTH DERBYSHIRE AREA.

TO NORTH DERBYSHIRE
MINEWORKERS
ABSENT FROM WORK

By the end of last week 65.6% of all NUM Industrial Workers
employed in the North Derbyshire Area had abandoned this futile strike.

Numbers by Main Local Authority locations* are as follows:

LOCATION	MEN ON BOOKS	AT WORK	%
Bolsover DC			
Bolsover Area	1049	775	74%
Glapwell	132	102	77%
Pleasley/New Houghton	276	84	30%
Shirebrook	1058	757	72%
Tibshelf/Blackwell	83	64	77%
South Normanton/Pinxton	117	90	77%
Whitwell/Barlborough/Clowne	690	332	48%
Chesterfield BC			
Chesterfield District	917	687	75%
Brimington/Staveley/Inkersall	1160	559	48%
N.E.Derbys. DC			
North Wingfield Area	291	219	75%
Clay Cross	257	150	58%
Unstone/Dronfield/Eckington/Renishaw	577	168	29%
Killamarsh	329	73	22%
Mickley/Stretton	106	82	77%
Calow/Duckmanton	351	220	63%
Wingerworth/Ashover	74	54	73%
Grassmoor/Hasland	376	233	62%
Mansfield District			
Mansfield/Mansfield Woodhouse	457	357	78%
Langwith/Langwith Junction	664	375	56%

Last week 7074 Derbyshire Miners received wages.

When are YOU coming back to work?

National Coal Board
NORTH DERBYSHIRE AREA
21st January, 1985

* The figures given above do not include mineworkers living outside the above districts.

TO NORTH DERBYSHIRE
MINEWORKERS
ABSENT FROM WORK

On Friday 25th January 1985,
7074 Derbyshire mineworkers will receive pay.

This represents 65.6% of all NUM Industrial Members employed in North Derbyshire Area

The numbers of NUM Industrial members at each unit are shown below

COLLIERY/UNIT	NUM ON BOOKS	NUM AT WORK		%
Arkwright	604	427	=	70.7%
High Moor	553	98	=	17.7%
Ireland	666	181	=	27.2%
Markham	2046	1252	=	61.2%
Renishaw Park	529	190	=	35.9%
Shirebrook	1947	1533	=	78.7%
Warsop	1174	911	=	77.6%
Whitwell	727	369	=	50.8%
Williamthorpe	274	248	=	90.5%
Duckmanton Workshops	581	431	=	74.2%
Blackwell Workshops	250	200	=	83.6%
Road Transport	154	129	=	83.8%
Other Activities	380	321	=	84.5%
Total Derbys. NUM	9885	6299	=	63.7%
Bolsover - Notts. NUM	896	775	=	86.5%
Total Area (NUM)	10781	7074	=	65.6%

On Monday day shift 21st January a further
184 NUM members returned to work.

When are YOU coming back to work?

Figure 6 An advertisement from the *Derbyshire Times* 25 January 1985. 'The campaign in North Derbyshire had been mounted with military precision; ordnance survey maps, pinned up at the office of the area headquarters, indicated the very streets and villages where miners lived.' Nicholas Jones *Strikes and the Media*.

Figure 7 *The Sun* MINE FUHRER page, prepared for publication on 15 May 1984 and, opposite, the edition as finally published.on 15 May.

THE Sun

Tuesday, May 15, 1984   16p   TODAY'S TV: PAGE 12

Sam ... and her vital assets

Sam's assets insured for £¼m

SUN EXCLUSIVE

By JOHN KAY

PAGE Three Samantha Fox is insured for whopper clauses — for a big figure could leave her speechless.

The tears on register for her assets on either leave her speechless.

So Samantha's agent asked insurance giant Lloyds to cover up with some suitable cover.

Under the five-year policy Samantha's assets will be insured against sagging, shrinking, health risks, or accidents.

Stunned

Agent Yvonne Paul said: "When we asked Lloyds if there was a chance there was a stunned silence.

"But they're now working out a percentage."

The amount Insurance men felt would be necessary to get

Continued on Page 3

Members of all The Sun production chapels refused to handle the Arthur Scargill picture and major headline on our lead story. The Sun has decided, reluctantly, to print the paper without either.

By CHARLES HAS and BRIAN DIXON

MINERS' leader Arthur Scargill gives a Hitler-style salute as he addresses his supporters at a mass rally yesterday.

The gesture was made by Mr Scargill as thousands of striking pitmen poured into Mansfield, Notts.

The big demo passed off peacefully — but after the miners' president left for his Sheffield headquarters a bloody flare-up left 20 hurt.

CLASHED

Miners spilled out of pubs at closing time and clashed violently with police.

Several officers were pelted by stones and bottles. Strikers were dragged to the ground.

And police staged mounted cavalry charges in

Continued on Page Four

£40,000 BINGO! Today's lucky numbers on Page 16

Figure 8 Leeds Postcards Sales and donations raised over £30,000 for the miners

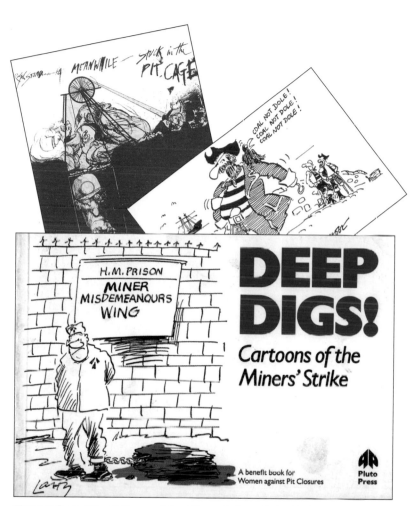

Figrue 9 *Deep Digs: Cartoons of the Miners Strike* published by Pluto Press 1985

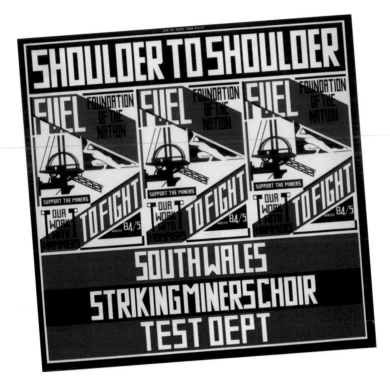

Figure 10 Album cover *Test Department* and *South Wales Striking Miners Choir*

Figure 11 *'Monday morning and shifting Everest* is really about my father. He was a ripper at Fryston when I was growing up and when I started there was working his way out, as was the thing with mining. You worked towards the face for the money then worked out as you got older. Anyway he would always get on about having to go to work and shift a load of muck as big as a house every day. It wasn't until I started there as a fitter and saw the men regularly doing this day in day out that I appreciated what he had to go through.' *Harry Malkin*

Figure 12 Press Gang

'I would see these press photographers each day at picket lines and rallies with arms full of cameras, lenses and rolls and rolls of film that I would have killed for! At the time, I could just about save enough money for one roll of film a week.'

Photograph: Ken Wilkinson

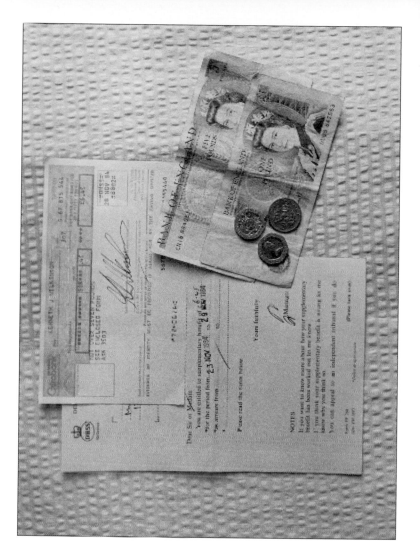

Figure 13 £6.45 a fortnight

'On 1st September 1984 I married my wife Lesley. Several weeks later we received a DHSS cheque for £6.45 a fortnight for the two of us to live on. The cheque was the first I had received as a striking miner since the start of the strike in March 1984. I had to borrow the money to take the photograph in order to record the event. However like many others we managed.'

Photograph: Ken Wilkinson

Figure 14 Alternative media from the miners' strike

Figures 15 & 16 Two photos by John Harris from Orgreave The first is the one of Leslie Boulton at Orgreave, the second, over page, taken by John Harris just after. Picture credits: John Harris/reportdigital.co.uk

»

Figure 17 Brenda Prince *The Battle of Orgreave*

'The reason I like this image is because it takes me back to an event which was essentially a class battle. I'd been covering the women's part in the miners' strike in Nottingham for over a year when I heard about a planned mass picket at Orgreave coke works. I left London very early in the morning and drove up with another photographer (John Sturrock) – it was exciting and I was full of anticipation. It was also frightening – especially when I saw the hundreds of policemen who had been bussed in from other forces. In order to protect myself from the police truncheons and the alsatian dogs they were setting onto miners - ordinary lads who were fighting for their jobs and livelihoods - I climbed a tree, from where I took this photograph. It reminds me of a cavalry charge. It was at Orgreave that I realised we are living in a police state.

Orgreave was a turning point in the miners' struggle and sadly they began to lose the fight. Thatcher and her government achieved what she set out to do – destroy the power of the miners' union and close down the pits. It is ironic that there is now talk of opening up new open-cast coalmines at the time of the so-called "credit crunch".' Brenda Prince, 2008

Figure 18 Striking miners at Kersley Colliery, Coventry eat in a soup kitchen funded by donations of fellow union members.

Figure 19 Arthur Scargill arrested at Orgreave picket line, 30 May 1984 Pictures: John Harris/reportdigital.co.uk

Figure 20 Mass picket at Thurcroft, South Yorkshire October 1984.

Figure 21 Miners' support group leads a demonstration of strikers at Rossington, South Yorkshire before the return to work at the end of the strike.

Pictures: John Harris/reportdigital.co.uk

Figure 22 Orgreave 30 May 1994
Figure 23 March in South Kirkby 16 March 1985 to commemorate the first anniversary of the death of David Jones on the picket line at Ollerton, Notts.
Pictures: John Sturrock

Figure 24 John Sturrock writes 'This photo was taken at an early morning picket line at Brodsworth pit north of Doncaster. It communicates something of the experience of the miners who faced the determination of the state to break their strike and consequentially their way of life. Coincidentally, this was the day of the bombing of the Grand Hotel in Brighton by the IRA, during the Tory Party conference'.

Figure 25 Keith Pattison

Figure 26 Keith Pattison

Keith Pattison: Twenty five years on, it comes as something of a shock to realize I only took a total of 7 frames for these two photographs.

I happened on the women with the push chair only as I ran to the miner's house I was staying in to hide the film that included the picture of the baby at the window (the police had a reputation for confiscating film). On the way I found this scene in a back street by the pit yard.

I had been in Easington Colliery, on the coast of County Durham, for a month or so, a johnny-come-lately to the strike, but opportune in that the quiet early months of the strike in the village were to be disrupted with a determined government push to bus willing miners into the pit.

I was, for want of a better phrase an 'artist in residence' with Easington Miners' Lodge, and spent the early days in the welfare lunch club and on picketing adventures to other pits. Threats of arrest were new to my innocence, threatened for no other reason than being alongside striking miners with a camera, rather than taking up the usual position with the local media on the opposite street corner.

I learned early on to welcome being surrounded by the largest miners I could find, and was touchingly taken care of as 'our photographer'. They felt aggrieved that a decidedly one-sided national media was reporting a fiction and that it was important that their history was recorded.

© Keith Pattison, 2008

Figure 27 'This picture was taken at the 1st national women's rally in support of striking miners, Barnsley Civic Hall, 12 May 1984'. Martin Jenkinson, 2008

Figure 28 Betty Cook above Woolley Edge colliery.

'This picture shows Betty Cook in February 1985 with her leg in plaster standing in a road above Woolley Colliery. Betty's knee had been smashed at 5.30 am the previous morning on the picket line by a policeman's baton. I immediately offered to drive her to hospital, but she had already promised to go to court to offer support to a miner's wife who had been arrested on a picket line the previous day. Loyalty came before her own suffering. Betty was someone with tremendous strength of character. It was 6 pm before she allowed me to drive her to hospital near Doncaster where she was treated for a broken kneecap'.

Photographer Raissa Page won the trust of mining communities in the Yorkshire pit towns of Bentley, Armthorpe and Barnsley where she stayed with miners and their families while photographing the strike. 'In such hard times, no one could have been more generous. Photographing the strike was a very humbling privilege. The amount of trust was one of the most precious things. I hope I never betrayed it,' she said. Picture: Raissa Page

Figure 29 Elicia Billingham and Betty Cook, Barnsley Miners' Wives Action Group with students at Hull University, February 1985 Photo Raissa Page

Figure 30 Coal and climate change. Leaflets for the Newcastle conference.

'It's just the *Sun* talking to itself again'

Figure 31 Ray Lowry died in October 2008. In *Media Hits The Pits*, published by the CPBF 1985, we see the anger and savage humour of his cartoons directed towards support for the miners' struggle. Ray's cartoons were absolutely right for the publication, capturing and exposing some of the absurdity in media claims of picket-line violence.

just incredibly touched by the dignity of the struggle. The mainstream press concentrated on Scargill and what he was doing, but when you went out on picket lines he was rarely mentioned. It was their struggle rather than his. We very rarely dwelt on anything Scargill was saying. We went out week after week. Once we were on the miners' side of the picket lines they were usually OK, we always used to take copies of the paper out with us. Sometimes we went through the whole gamut of pickets being fed at the miners' club at three o'clock in the morning before going out picketing.

We did report on the issues of 'uneconomic' pits and so on, we informed the discussion, we weren't just reporting it as the working class against the state. We homed in on those mining communities being a way of life, a culture in themselves, and that was something being lost. All right, there might be all sorts of aspects of that culture you don't like, but there was something that was holding them together and the best bits of which you needed to preserve.'

Such alternative journalism included:

— Publishing diary-style reports from picket lines and soup kitchens.

— Analysing arguments around economics, clean coal technology, and combined heat and power.

— Exposing how the benefits system was being used to increase hardship among strikers' families.

— Scrutinising the role of the police and of elected politicians (often Labour) on 'sleeping' police committees.

— Reporting in detail from trials of arrested miners, including after the strike when most other media had lost interest.

As important as such heavyweight reporting and analysis were the interviews, photographs and poems that gave voice to people who were being caricatured elsewhere as Scargill's gullible foot soldiers, and that demonstrated their humanity in all its complexity. There was humour too, as when a miner commented on the Coal Board's latest 'back to work' figures: 'There's so many ghosts going into our pit that we're not going to picket anymore, we're going to get a priest on the gate to exorcise them.' (*LOP*, 7 December 1984.)

The role played by mainstream media was seen as key from the early days of the strike, as in a story headlined: Media & State combine to thwart Miners (ps it seems like it's a class war):

'Tempers flared on Monday afternoon this week, when a thousand Yorkshire miners gathered outside the Barnsley offices of their union. Some fights broke out between miners and TV camera crews, and between miners and police...

The miners feel that the media have distorted the issues involved in the dispute, which is about pit closures, so that it now centres on the issues of a national ballot and flying picketing... Despite all its interest in the 'legality' or otherwise of flying picketing, there has been little media interest in examining the 'legality' or otherwise of flying police roadblocks, hundreds of miles from the coalfields.'

(*LOP*, 23 March 1984.)

Distorted or blinkered coverage in most of the mainstream media, most of the time, was a recurrent theme in alternative media. That was hardly surprising. After all, alternative media had been created as a do-it-yourself critique of mainstream media. Crucially, it was a critique conducted in practice – by creating alternatives – rather than merely in theory.

Countering the 'lie machine'

The role of mainstream media featured prominently in the *Miners' Campaign Tapes*, a series of short films distributed on VHS video cassettes during the strike by an alternative film network. One, entitled *The Lie Machine*, dissected some of the ways in which so much of the mainstream print and broadcast media effectively sided with the Thatcher government during the dispute. Among those featured were *Daily Mirror* journalist Paul Foot, Dennis Skinner MP, Mike Power of the printers' union NGA, and groups of men and women from mining communities. In addition to highlighting media inconsistencies – including the demonising of Arthur Scargill as a madman with a twitching eye that somehow never twitched(!) and a TV news script about 'pickets charging police' when footage clearly showed mounted police actually charging the miners – the film briefly examined the economic interests of the newspaper owners who were so hostile to the strike. It also found time to mention the rare cases of printers using their own trade union muscle to achieve more balanced coverage for the miners, before concluding that the best way of becoming informed was to read non-mainstream papers such as the *Morning Star* and the NUM's own journal the *Miner*. *The Miner* was widely distributed and strikers at some pits even produced their own publications, such as the *Tannoy* at Ledston Luck in Yorkshire.

The *Miners Campaign Tape Project* was the product of a network of independent film workshops including Active Image (Sheffield), Amber Films (Newcastle), Cardiff Community Video Workshop, Edinburgh Film Workshop, Films at Work (London), London Video Arts, Nottingham Video Project, Platform Films (London), and Trade Films (Gateshead). These workshops, many of which relied on funding from the relatively new Channel 4 television channel, worked together with members of the technicians' trade union ACTT and the National Union of Journalists to produce a series of short, sharp videos that were endorsed by the mineworkers' union. However, although the tapes won official union backing, they were not megaphones for union leaders or bureaucrats; far more prominent were the voices of rank and file miners and their supporters, including the women of the coalfields who became so crucial to efforts to sustain the strike. One tape was called *Not Just Tea and Sandwiches – miners' wives speak out.*

Writing in *The Alternative Media Handbook* in 2007, Alan Fountain[2] recalled their impact:

'The tapes were made with the objective of winning
and consolidating support for the strike and to serve
as a means of fundraising to help the strikers and their
families fight for the future of their communities… The
tapes were distributed by Trade Films in Gateshead
and Platform Films in London, through miners'
lodges, other trades unions and various support groups
and individuals…The response to the tapes was
overwhelming. Over 4,000 were distributed in the UK.
Internationally the tapes went to France, Germany,
Australia, Denmark, Sweden, Italy, Ireland, the USA, the
Netherlands, Greece, Canada and Belgium and raised
considerable money for the miners and their families. A
two-week tour of Australia raised £20,000 and Danish
dockers who dubbed Danish voices over the tapes raised
£40,000.'

Recognition in the mining communities and the wider working class was most important, but the tapes also won the 1985 John Grierson Award, named in honour of the pioneering documentary director. Commending the award, the CPBF's Julian Petley wrote in *Broadcast*[3] magazine:

'What the Miners Campaign Video Tapes show…is just
how much can be achieved without the conventional
broadcast media at all. If television consistently ignores or
misrepresents those in conflict with the state…then they
in turn will increasingly ignore and distrust mainstream
television and start looking to the alternatives offered by
the new technology.'

A quarter of a century on and Petley – now professor

of film and television at Brunel University – recalls: 'The films ranged from straight agitprop to more aesthetically sophisticated styles of documentary and they did a wonderful job raising awareness and money. But we should remember that they wouldn't have been possible without Channel 4 because it funded the workshops, which was one of C4's most important achievements.'

Conclusion: back to the future?

In 1985, Alan Fountain[4] – then C4's commissioning editor for independent film and video - described the tapes as 'one of the most impressive examples of oppositional media activity during the strike' and argued that they could be a model for others to follow: 'Close links with independent programme makers have certainly benefited the union during the strike, and the construction of such relationships is an important task for the labour movement in future. So too is the possibility of establishing a significant videotape production and distribution network working on behalf of the labour movement.'

That never happened to any significant extent, although Trade Films produced 18 video editions of *Northern Newsreel*, covering union and social issues from an alternative perspective. Their final tape in 1991 looked back to media coverage of the miners' strike with a deconstruction of a TV news bulletin, courtesy of the Glasgow University Media Group. It also featured the CPBF's (relatively fresh-faced) Granville Williams and Tony Lennon analysing trends in media ownership; an issue that remains critical today, when mainstream media offer such a narrow range of perspectives despite the illusion of greater choice.

The cold hand of Thatcherism that inflicted so much social and economic damage on the coalfields eventually impacted upon alternative media projects too. Many independent film and video workshops ceased to exist when their funding was cut.

Most print alternatives neither sought nor obtained grants as their means of production was cheaper than for film, but they depended on free labour, sometimes augmented by money earned from printing or typesetting for groups within the alternative sphere. Supplies of income and labour became less plentiful as the political and economic climate grew harsher, and the defeat of the strike itself left many alternative media activists burned out or demoralised. Although there followed some high-profile successes (*Wapping Post*) and failures (*News on Sunday*), by the time the eighties had become the nineties the tide had gone out on a lot of social, political and cultural activities and movements. The networks that had sustained alternative media such as the local papers that gathered in Leeds in 1984, or the workshops that produced the miners' tapes, had been damaged if not destroyed.

But different circumstances and different generations suggest different alternatives. In 1994 a group of environmental activists and frustrated TV producers combined to launch a series of video bulletins called *Undercurrents*, which reported on and for the growing eco warrior scene. And then came the internet, which is where *Undercurrents'* footage can be viewed today, along with alternatives ranging from the Indymedia network and the feminist website F-Word to the so-called blogosphere, via print/online hybrids such as *Red Pepper* and *SchNews*.

From Chartist newspapers to the miners' strike and beyond, radical and alternative media have always tended to be short-lived. Titles come and go, conditions change and new technologies emerge, but the reasons for the creation of such media do not go away. Alternative media continue to exist in different forms today, sharing many of the attitudes of alternative media that were around in 1984-5. It is a pity that so much contemporary alternative media seems to eschew the sort of reportage and investigation that could be found during the miners' strike, in favour of commentary and opinion, but who knows what the future holds? By keeping alive a form of collective memory about what has been, publications such as the one you are reading now help us to imagine what can still be. And, as the 1984 alternative papers conference put it, small need not mean insignificant.

Notes

1   For the pamphlet *A Northern Star*, by Tony Harcup published by Campaign for Press and Broadcasting Freedom 1994.

2   Kate Coyer, Tony Dowmunt and Alan Fountain, *Alternative Media Handbook*, London: Routledge, 2007.

3   'Doing without the broadcast media' by Julian Petley, *Broadcast*, 28 June 1985.

4   Alan Fountain 'The Miners and Television' in *Digging Deeper* edited by Huw Beynon. London: Verso 1985.

The miners and the secret state
Robin Ramsay

In his 1987 book *Spycatcher* former MI5 officer Peter Wright revealed one of MI5's biggest secrets; but focused as we were on his comments about the plotting against Harold Wilson, we didn't initially notice the section on page 175 where he wrote that the Communist Party of Great Britain (CPGB)'s 'Reuben Falber... had recently been made cashier of the Russian funds.' Wright tells us that MI5 planned to burgle Falber's flat in search of the files detailing the payments but their plan failed – and he leaves it there. To MI5 in 1958 the proof of the 'Moscow gold' must have had something of the status of the Holy Grail and Wright apparently wanted us to believe that aware that the CPGB were getting actual cash money from the Soviets, MI5 were either unable to detect the payoffs in London, or, having made one failed attempt, just gave up. This is simply not credible.[1] The point is that MI5 knew about the 'Moscow gold' and said nothing about it. Had the existence of Soviet funding been revealed in the late 1950s, the CPGB would have been irreparably damaged. But for MI5 this 'secret" link to the Soviet Union was too useful a tool for use against the left in the UK, particularly the Labour Party. In effect MI5 let the CPGB run as a honey trap for the British left: anyone who made contact with it, supported it, or wrote for it, could be legitimately investigated as they were in touch with a body funded by an 'enemy power'.[2]

In 1984, 36 years after MI5 first discovered the 'Moscow gold', this Soviet 'trace' provided the British secret state with the justification to undertake full-scale offensive operations against the leadership of the NUM. As NUM president Arthur Scargill had been a member of the Young Communist League, and was trying to set up an international mineworkers body with representatives of the mineworkers' unions of the Soviet bloc, vice-president the late Mick McGahey, was a member of the CPGB, and general secretary Peter Heathfield's then wife, the late Betty Heathfield, had been a member of the CPGB, it wasn't hard for the secret state to present this as a communist conspiracy.

In charge of MI5's operation against the NUM, then the head of its F2 branch, Stella Rimington, wrote later:

'The 1984 miners' strike was supported by a very large number of members of the National Union of Mineworkers, but it was directed by a triumvirate who had declared that they were using the strike to try to bring down the elected government of Margaret Thatcher and it was actively supported by the Communist party. What was it legitimate for us to do about that? We quickly decided that the activities of picket lines and miners' wives' support groups were not our concern, even though they were of great concern to the police who had to deal with the law-and-order aspects of the strike; accusations that we were running agents or telephone interceptions to get advance warning of picket movements are wrong. We in MI5 limited our investigations to the activities of those who were using the strike for subversive purposes.' [3]

A year later she added to that account:

'The leaders of the miners' strike themselves had actually said that one of the purposes of the miners' strike was to overthrow Mrs Thatcher who was the elected Prime Minister of the country and the industrial department of the Communist Party was very involved in all sorts of different ways in the strike and that was of concern to us, that's what we were interested in.' [4]

Rimington's central proposition is false: the CPGB and its industrial department did not support the strike at all, much to the disgust of many of its members. In 2005 Arthur Scargill said: 'We had a number of people and industries that deliberately betrayed the miners. For example, the

Communist Party bears a heavy responsibility for what took place. They were pushing from day one for the strike to be called off.' [5]

Rimington denies that MI5 was running agents, which may be technically true: police Special Branches ran the agents; but they reported to MI5. [6] Rimington denies running telephone intercepts, which may also be true. *Guardian* journalists were told by employees of GCHQ that, with its larger partner the NSA, GCHQ was surveilling the NUM and its attempts to hide its resources from state sequestration. (Again the Soviet 'trace' would justify this.) [7]

The role of encouraging strikebreaking was taken up by the private sector and the politicians: David Hart, residing in a suite at Claridge's Hotel, backed by Mrs Thatcher and funded by persons unknown, spread money and personnel around the non-striking miners. Local police forces, supplemented by the Metropolitan Police, did the crowd control/strikebreaking duties among the pits. [8]

The operations by the British secret state against the NUM in 1984/5 were the climax of almost two decades in which the growing presence of the left in politics and trade unions was met, investigated, surveilled and countered by an alliance of politicians, employers' organisations, anti-communist and anti-socialist trade union officials, and state officials in what we might call an anti-subversion network. In 1964, when Labour won the general election, this network consisted of: the Economic League and the Aims of Industry; MI5 and local police Special Branches; the state's anti-communist research-propaganda-psy-ops outfit, the Information Research Department (IRD); IRD's media assets; anti-communist groups in the labour movement, most obviously Common Cause and its off shoot, Industrial Research and Information Services (IRIS); US London embassy employees, usually labour attachés, and the CIA; and parts of the Labour Party's organisation, the party agent network and the Organisation

Subcommittee. [9]

In 1964 Labour was in office for the first time since Attlee. And the Left grew and industrial conflict grew. Wilson and Barbara Castle tried to reduce the unions' power with the *In Place of Strife* proposals, but were seen off by the unions and the Parliamentary Labour left. Labour lost the election in 1970. In came Edward Heath who wanted to turn Britain into West Germany, with membership of the EEC, and a semi-corporate state in which the trade unions are embraced by the state in exchange for influence (essentially the same thing that Harold Wilson and Barbara Castle sought). The trade unions resisted this embrace (registration under the Industrial Relations Act) and industrial conflict grew. The 'flying pickets' of the Yorkshire NUM famously prevented the police from keeping open the Saltley coke depot in 1972. In 1974 Heath called a 'Who rules Britain?' election and lost.

Industrial militancy had apparently won a famous victory. But the NUM's success at Saltley also produced a major expansion of MI5's F branch, which monitored the left.

The wider public-private anti-subversion lobby believed (some members more seriously than others) that at the heart of the rising industrial militancy in Britain was the Communist Party of Great Britain, and particularly its industrial department, referred to by Stella Rimington above; and that the CPGB was an agent of the Soviet Union. To this theory of Soviet influence the Communist Party contributed by occasionally boasting of its influence on the Labour Party left; and the Labour Party itself unwittingly added the final touch in 1973 by abolishing the Proscription List of organisations – mostly 1950s Soviet fronts of no political significance and what were then tiny Trotskyist groups – that Labour Party members could not join. Look, said the anti-subversion network, this shows that the communists are in control of the Labour Party!

Part of the anti-subversion network took seriously claims

from MI5 and CIA counterintelligence officers that Harold Wilson might be a KGB agent (though they had no evidence for this other than the suspicion of a Soviet defector). Thus among the network's members there was the picture of a trade union movement manipulated if not run by the Soviet-funded CPGB and a Labour Party, in turn funded largely by the trade unions, headed by someone who might be a Soviet stooge.[10]

Labour took office again in 1974 and there followed two years of talks of coups, surveillance, disinformation and smears against members of the Labour government, climaxing with Wilson's retirement.[11] In the midst of this Mrs Thatcher became leader of the Conservative Party, was briefed by the anti-subversion network and apparently took on board the Soviet conspiracy theory. Her use of the expression 'the enemy within' about the NUM was a barely coded nod to the anti-subversion network.[12] In the final paragraph of the 30 pages on the NUM strike in her bland memoir, *The Downing Street Years*, she wrote: 'What the strike's defeat established was that Britain could not be made ungovernable by the Fascist Left.' (p.378) In *The Enemy Within* (pp 18/19) Seamus Milne quotes an unnamed chief constable as saying that he had been told by a Home Office official that Mrs Thatcher was 'convinced that a secret communist cell around Scargill was orchestrating the strike in order to bring down the country.'

With 'one of them' now leading the Conservative Party, the anti-subversion lobby began operations against the trade unions – notably at Grunwick – and helped to set-up the Freedom Association.

Winning the election in 1979, the Thatcher faction of the Conservative Party began preparing for a showdown with what they saw as the heart of the communist conspiracy in Britain, the NUM. Thanks to the existence of the 'Moscow gold', kept secret by MI5, the secret state had the perfect pretext to use all its resources against the miners.

The end of the strike did not end the operations against the NUM's leading officials. In 1990 an elaborate disinformation operation was mounted to portray Arthur Scargill and Peter Heathfield as personally corrupt. Two employees of the NUM at the time of the strike, Roger Windsor and Steve Hudson, and a Libyan living in England, were used to state that Scargill and Heathfield had used funds from Libya – in cash – to pay the mortgages on their houses during the strike. This story was run initially in the *Daily Mirror* and on TV by *The Cook Report*. Neither bothered to check one basic fact: did Scargill and Heathfield actually have mortgages? They didn't; and twelve years later, editor of the *Mirror* at the time, Roy Greenslade, apologised to Scargill and Heathfield for running the false story. In his account Greenslade describes how initially he wondered if the story was some kind of operation by the British state: the only witness the Mirror had to the transfer of the Libyan money was Roger Windsor, NUM chief executive at the time. (The Libyan, Abassi, merely confirmed that Libyan money had been given to the NUM, not how it had been dispersed.) But Greenslade's doubts disappeared when a second NUM employee, a former NUM finance officer, Steve Hudson, confirmed Windsor's account of money being counted out and given to Scargill and Heathfield. Greenslade wrote:

> 'Out of the blue, Steve Hudson, the finance officer whom Windsor had named as the other man in the room when the money was counted out, phoned one of our reporters. Hours later, he turned up in my office to give a taped interview in which he confirmed every word of Windsor's account. He didn't ask for payment and spoke under no duress.'

Ah, the logic of the tabloid journalist: he didn't ask for money, so he must be telling the truth. (The fact that Roger Windsor was eventually paid a total of £80,000 by the *Mirror* does not seem to have raised a doubt about his veracity in

Greenslade's mind.)

Here we have a recognisable and quite elaborate disinformation operation. But by whom? We don't know. Most suspect MI5. Stella Rimington was asked about Roger Windsor and MI5 and gave a very curious reply: 'It would be correct to say that he, Roger Windsor, was never an agent in any sense of the word that you can possibly imagine.'

This baroque variation on the non-denial denial merely confirmed the suspicions. But like her specific denial that MI5 ran agents quoted above, this might be technically true: Special Branch, who did run agents and reported to MI5, might have been running this (although it would be way off their normal range of known activities if they were).

But it could be another agency. It might not even be British one. Since the NUM leaders had been trying to form an international miners' organisation with union leaders of the Soviet bloc, the CIA, for example, which has tried to control European labour since 1945, would have been interested. We don't know; and we may never know. But an operation it was and it conned the British media. [13]

Notes

1 Falber admitted his role in 1991 after details of the Soviet payments were found in files in Moscow.

2 How did MI5 know about the Soviet funds to the CPGB? Perhaps through their penetration of the CPGB, though the knowledge of the money was held very closely within the Party. Perhaps through Morris Childs, the American Communist Party's link with the Soviets, their bagman, who was an FBI agent. On Childs see, for example a summary of the major book on this subject at <http://findarticles.com/p/articles/mi_m1282/is_n4_v48/ai_18111844> and see also <http://www.theatlantic.com/doc/200207/garrow>, an essay by David Garrow who first discovered Morris Childs' role with the FBI.

3 Stella Rimington, 'Peter Wright and Harold Wilson', *The Guardian*, 11

September 2001.

4 <*http://news.bbc.co.uk/nol/shared/spl/hi/programmes/true_spies/ transcripts/ truespies_prog2.txt*>

5 <*http://www.anphoblacht.com/news/detail/8342*> See also CBGP member Graham Stevenson's account of the internal politics of the CPGB at the time of the strike at <*http://www.grahamstevenson.me.uk/ archives/000047. html]*

6 See <*http://news.bbc.co.uk/1/hi/programmes/true_spies/2351547.stm*> for an account by former Special Branch officers of recruiting informants among the NUM and <*http://www.guardian.co.uk/politics/2002/nov/01/uk.military*> for an account of Special Branch's agent in the NUM leadership.

7 Seamus Milne, *The Enemy Within*, Verso 1994, p 258.

8 There were many rumours at the time of soldiers being drafted in as civilians but none of these stories have been stood up.

9 On IRD see Paul Lasmar and James Oliver, *Britain's Secret Propaganda War 1948-77*, Stroud, Gloucester: Sutton. 1998. On some of the American influences see Hugh Wilford, *The CIA, the British Left and the Cold War*, London: Frank Cass. 2003. The only overview of the network still appears to be my 1996 'The Clandestine Caucus' which is available at the *Lobster* website *(www.lobster-magazine.co.uk)* though this needs updating in places.

10 This theory was articulated by journalists such as Chapman Pincher of the *Daily Express* and can be seen in his *Inside Story*, London: Sidgwick and Jackson, 1977.

11 This is discussed in detail in Stephen Dorril and Robin Ramsay, *Smear! Wilson and the Secret State* London: Fourth Estate. 1991. Though some of the anti-subversion network suspected they might have driven Wilson out of office the truth was more banal: his father had what we now call Alzeimer's disease and Wilson suspected he might get it and resigned before it developed.

12 One of the network's leading figures, Brian Crozier, who worked for the CIA and IRD, describes briefing Mrs Thatcher in his memoir, *Free Agent*, London: HarperCollins, 1993, pp 131-133.

13 The operation is the subject matter of Seamus Milne's excellent *The Enemy Within*, London: Verso. 1994 and 1995.

The soul searching of a former BBC correspondent
Nicholas Jones

Just like the sustained scare story over weapons of mass destruction which preceded the war against Iraq, the year-long pit dispute was played out against an equally well-entrenched narrative aimed in this case at demonising the 'enemy within'. For the British news media, the confrontation between Margaret Thatcher and Arthur Scargill had as much potency as the fight to the finish with Saddam Hussein. Many journalists have reflected ruefully on the way they were taken in by the pro-war propaganda of George Bush and Tony Blair in the months leading up to the US offensive in March 2003 and similarly when I think back to my reporting of the 1984-5 strike I have to admit that in the end I got ensnared by the seeming inevitability of the Thatcherite story line that the mineworkers had to be defeated in order to smash trade union militancy.

With the benefit of hindsight, and the subsequent evidence of a vindictive pit closure programme which continued during the decade which followed the strike, perhaps the news media should own up to a collective failure of judgement comparable to that during the build-up to the Iraq war. As most journalists have since acknowledged, not enough was done to question the pre-war intelligence so as to determine the true nature of the threat posed by Iraq's chemical and biological weapons and likewise the same charge could perhaps be levelled against the industrial and labour correspondents of the 1980s.

My erstwhile colleagues might not agree with my conclusion but I do not think any of us ever imagined that such was the Conservatives' contempt for the National Coal Board, and so great was the Thatcherite fear and hatred of the National Union of Mineworkers, that the Tories would end up all but destroying the British coal industry and marginalising a valuable source of energy. Perhaps we should have been more sceptical. For my own part, I probably took it for granted that the Conservatives still believed that coal had a future once the uneconomic pits had been closed and I certainly did not suspect that the Tories would force through a closure programme which would exceed even the direst predictions of the NUM President about the existence of a hidden 'hit list'.

To Scargill and many union activists the dividing line could not have been clearer: journalists were part and parcel of the class enemy and he always predicted they would instinctively support Thatcher. That charge was reinforced in April 2004 during events to mark the 20th anniversary of the strike when, in his role as the union's honorary president, Scargill accused the news media of trying to rewrite events by denying that it had been 'the most principled struggle in British trade union history'.

While I would contend that broadcasters like myself tried valiantly to represent both sides of the dispute, we did have to work within what had become an all-powerful narrative: the country could not afford to continue subsidising uneconomic coal mines, devastating though that might be for their communities; the strike itself was a denial of democracy because there had been no pit head ballot and the violence on the miners' picket lines, by challenging the rule of law, constituted a threat to the democratic government of the country.

In the final months of the strike, once it became clear there was no longer any chance of a negotiated settlement, the balance of coverage tipped almost completely in the management's favour. And therefore I do accept, as *Media Hits The Pits* subsequently argued, that most radio and television journalists became, in effect, the cheerleaders for the return to work. By then the narrative had progressed to a much simpler story line: the outcome would depend on the NCB's success in persuading miners to abandon the strike and rejoin their pits. The media's attention was focussed on the 'new faces' who were going back to work. For the newspapers these men were the heroes; television pictures, filmed from behind police lines, showed them being bussed into their pits, braving the pickets. The news agenda had been turned to the government's advantage. Once the NCB could claim that half the men were back at work, Mrs Thatcher would declare victory, as eventually she did.

Had we known then that defeat of the NUM would not suffice and that the Conservatives would accelerate the plunder of North Sea gas reserves for power generation rather than sustain a viable coal industry, perhaps we might have done far more at the time to have scrutinised the government's true intentions and highlighted both the remarkable solidarity of the pit villages and the threat which the closures posed to the cohesion of their communities.

Wilful destruction of great industries and their workforces was rapidly turning Thatcher into a hate figure in Britain's industrial heartlands and that shared sense of loss finally crossed the class divide within months of John Major's re-election as Prime Minister in 1992 when Michael Heseltine announced unexpectedly that because of falling demand for coal from the privatised electricity industry, British Coal would have to close thirty one of the fifty pits that remained in operation and shed another 30,000 jobs. Despite all that the miners had done to improve efficiency, the 'dash for gas' presented a cheaper option. As my own researches confirmed at the time, it had slowly dawned on British Coal's management that the industry itself and the public at large had been hoodwinked: viable pits would have to be closed simply because it was more cost effective in the short term to build new gas-fired rather than the more expensive coal-fired power stations. There had been similar consternation before the privatisation of British Gas in 1986 when to the dismay of the then chairman, Sir Denis Rooke, the Conservatives first encouraged the use of natural gas to generate electricity rather than conserve it as a premium fuel for household use.

While the complexities surrounding the competing price structures of coal, gas and electricity passed most people by there was a general recognition that the public had been misled and the unfairness of what was happening was plain to see: the pits were being decimated out of political and commercial expediency. By then consciences had been well and truly stirred in the prosperous south east of England and the miners' plight had come to symbolise the growing unease over the social cost of wanton industrial vandalism. When the NUM organised a march through London to coincide with a critical House of Commons vote on the Heseltine closure programme it attracted 100,000 protesters and drew support from across the capital; twice as many attended the TUC's mass rally in Hyde Park the following Sunday.

Even though I have spent much of my career trying to keep abreast of the highs and lows of the coal industry, I found it a humbling experience digging into my files and turning over the newspaper front pages for 22 and 26 October 1992. If only the miners and their union had been able to win over the right-wing press in the way they did that week, Mrs Thatcher might well have been forced to negotiate her way out the strike.

Almost filling *The Sun*'s front page was a photograph of 'a mighty army of miners' whose march for coal and jobs 'won the support of Britain's diehard Tories'. To the paper's evident surprise even 'Sloane Rangers left their tables at swanky eateries and customers poured from posh boutiques in Kensington and Chelsea to wave them on'. Instead of the invective of the 1980s, the Sun's editorial reflected the mood on the streets: 'The miners' conduct yesterday was exemplary. They are men of honour'. For the *Daily Mail* it had been a day of 'quiet dignity' when the miners and their families brought their 'peaceful protest to London' in 'marked contrast to the ugly, violent scenes which characterised the 1984 strike'.

Six Conservative MPs voted against the government and others abstained, cutting the government's majority to thirteen, but although Heseltine promised a further review and a temporary reprieve for ten pits, the protests ultimately proved futile as the closures went ahead. None the less it begged the question: if it was possible to force the Major government on to the defensive through the combined pressure of two demonstrations, a backbench revolt and a critical media, why had the NUM been unable to mobilise that same level of support when it mattered most of all in 1984?

By the early 1990s the prism through which the miners were being reported had changed dramatically. Strikes were no longer regarded as the threat they had been at the start of the Thatcher decade; privatisation of state-owned enterprises had weakened national pay bargaining in many key industries; and union membership had halved. But more importantly the media's narrative had turned decisively against the Conservatives and it was far easier for the NUM to win public sympathy. Mrs Thatcher had been ousted after the fiasco of the poll tax and despite winning the 1992 general election, John Major's political standing had been shattered by the Black Wednesday debacle of British withdrawal from the European exchange rate mechanism.

While it was of no long-term comfort to the miners, their sympathetic treatment almost a decade after the strike illustrated the ever-changing focus of the news agenda and the all important part it can play. I share the conclusion reached by the authors of *Media Hits The Pits* that the role of the mass media 'was not itself decisive to the final outcome' of the 1984-5 strike but I do think that if the media's near-unanimous narrative had not been so hostile to the NUM and had instead done more to challenge the government, then Mrs Thatcher might well have been forced to reach a negotiated settlement during the initial phase of the dispute.

Again, with the benefit of hindsight, it is clear that what became a make or break strike for the trade union movement, was being conducted during a period of unprecedented expansion in the media which in turn was having a profound effect on the way news was being reported. Breakfast-time television was building up its audience after being launched by BBC and TV-AM in 1983; there was new investment in regional television programming; local radio stations were opening up across the country; and the national newspapers, which were benefiting from increased advertising revenue, had more editorial space to give to columnists and commentators.

News bulletins and discussion programmes were available morning, noon and night providing a non-stop national and local arena for information, comment and opinion. Trade union leaders who had previously shunned the media, believing they could rely solely on the movement's industrial strength, were having to come to terms with the impact of 24/7 reporting and the way powerful forces could manipulate the news agenda and influence the all-important narrative that framed the day's coverage.

Such was the strength of the Thatcherite story line against the NUM that it became all-embracing. Newspaper proprietors were only too keen to ensure Scargill and the miners were defeated, hoping no doubt it would be of help in their own subsequent confrontation with the print unions (and within months of the NUM's defeat Rupert Murdoch began recruiting alternative print workers for his new plant at Wapping). While traditionally the left had been able to ignore the right-wing press and appeal directly to the membership for solidarity, the anti-union propaganda was proving to be far more pervasive than in previous disputes because the narrative was beginning to be joined up across the output of the many new and competing media outlets.

A review of the morning papers had become a vital

component of the breakfast television programmes providing a new and expanding showcase for newspaper front pages. More often than not the headlines and pictures tended to highlight picket-line violence, lavish praise on the working miners and demonise Scargill. Opinionated columnists were given free rein to adopt highly partisan positions which were reflected in the radio and television coverage and often provoked further controversy on the daily talk shows and phone-ins. Expanded news bulletins over breakfast, at lunchtime and in the early evening gave correspondents extra air time to give a running commentary on the combined efforts of the NCB, government and police to thwart the pickets and break the strike.

Scargill was no mean opponent in reaching out to journalists and often, single-handed, he managed to command the attention of Fleet Street and the radio and television news rooms. But his skill in projecting himself masked the failure of the miners' union to devise a communications strategy to counter the far superior news management being orchestrated on behalf of the government by advertising and public relations consultants. Scargill's repeated declaration that the media should be regarded as the enemy played into Mrs Thatcher's hands. Reporters were simply not welcome in numerous pit villages and such was the hostility towards television crews that they had little alternative but to seek protection behind police lines where they had a greater chance of obtaining the all-important footage of the latest 'new faces' abandoning the strike.

Once corralled in this way, television crews and photographers were as limited in what they could observe as embedded reporters were in the Iraq War. Radio and television coverage of the latter stages of the miners' strike provided a foretaste of what has become the Achilles heel of the modern news media. If the opportunities to take pictures are restricted and there is a dearth of new information, broadcasters may find they have no alternative but to live with a degree of distortion rather than have nothing else to offer listeners and viewers. Given the increased competition, constant demand for new images and ever-tighter deadlines, it is no longer an option to say that nothing has happened. Come what may, news bulletins have to be updated.

I quite accept that the media could have done far more to reflect the positive side of the 1984-5 dispute and the breadth of support from across the country for the miners and their families, whether it was street collections, deliveries of food, clothes and toys or countless other acts of solidarity. However, help often had to be given without public recognition for fear of attracting the attention of the police and the organisers did not want their clandestine efforts to be publicised.

Nevertheless one positive legacy of the troubled relationship between journalists and NUM activists is that no union has ever repeated the mistake of alienating a group of reporters assigned to cover a strike. Recent fire fighters' disputes have provided a telling illustration of media awareness. Whenever possible television reporters seized the chance to conclude their reports with a piece-to-camera filmed from outside a fire station. The brazier would always be well alight; the flames would help light up the shot; and standing around in a dignified way would be fire fighters carrying placards in support of their wage claim. The FBU had learned a valuable lesson: let the pictures help tell the story.

The decade I spent reporting industrial and trade union affairs had a profound effect on my outlook and, without doubt, the year-long pit dispute was the most momentous assignment during a fifty year career. Reporters rarely indulge in soul searching but I freely admit that what has troubled me most of all was coverage of the miners' struggle and the minimal editorial scrutiny of the subsequent ruination of their once great industry. Although industrial and labour reporting commands nothing like the attention it once did, I hope the

25th anniversary of the strike will encourage a reflective mood on the part of the media and a recognition that any thoughts which journalists might have harboured at the time about the Conservative government's good faith towards the future of the coal industry were tragically misplaced.

The making of an icon – and how the British press tried to destroy it
Michael Bailey and Julian Petley

Orgreave in Yorkshire became a focal point of the strike because of British Steel's use of lorry convoys to transport coking coal from there to its Scunthorpe steel works.

Orgreave was an attempt by the government, through the deployment of highly trained riot police, to prove to the miners and trade unionists at large that picketing could not succeed. For the miners it was a chance to turn the tide of the strike. To hit an economic target and provide a focus around which trade unionists could mobilise in support ... The last great battle at Orgreave was on 18 June 1984 when 5000 pickets in teeshirts and trainers were confronted by a similar number of policemen with riot shields backed by dogs and horses. The government knew they had won a round. Negotiations with the NUM were suddenly broken off. Thatcher had tasted blood. *The Economist* noted 'the government wants to be seen to have broken the legendary power of the miners'. (*Blood, Sweat and Tears*, Artworker Books, 1985).

Lesley Boulton was at Orgreave that day, supporting the striking miners.
Lesley Boulton: A friend and I drove to Orgreave and we parked in the Asda car park. We got there about 10am and it was a gloriously sunny day ... miners and sympathisers were getting drinks and food from the supermarket, playing football in the car park and slowly making their way down to a field over the bridge. By the time we got down to the field it was quite busy with smatterings of miners dotted here and there, just sitting around talking and having a laugh. Many had their shirts off and were making the most of the good weather. So, the miners and supporters like myself were, on the whole, very relaxed and there was no sense of what was

to come; nobody expected that the day would turn into this horrific, violent confrontation. The miners clearly weren't planning a battle – men don't go into battle with their shirts tucked into their back pockets! The police, on the other hand, were stood in massed ranks, many dressed in full riot gear. It was very odd, almost like they were actually wanting something to happen. They weren't prepared simply for the possibility of violence. Of course, we now know that the police had been instructed by their political masters that this was the day to show the miners what was what and who was who. It was showdown time and the police were spoiling for a fight. It was time to show the hoi polloi who was in control, even if it meant the police had to kick the shit out of them. When it eventually kicked off, the police charged up the field, the miners retreated into the village, and both the miners and police set up barricades. A small group of miners started throwing stones and the police charged them, at which point I dived behind a wall and I came out only when they'd gone. I then started walking down to the bus stop; just before it was a short wall and behind the wall was an injured miner who looked to have cracked ribs and was clearly in a lot of pain. I was really concerned and I asked a policeman who was stood in the street to get an ambulance, at which point a mounted policeman came out of nowhere, swinging his truncheon at me. I only just managed to get out of the way thanks to a miner who pulled me to one side. And that's exactly what John Harris captured on film. The police were clearly enjoying themselves … they were excited, out of control … it felt a bit like Peterloo but without the swords.

John Harris was a young photographer covering the strike for the International Freelance Library (IFL).
John Harris: During the previous mass pickets at Orgreave, the police had corralled all the photographers so that they couldn't see what was going on. So on the day on which I

took the photograph of Lesley we'd decided to take the risk
of going in with the miners. The previous week I'd been told
off by my boss at IFL, Simon Guttman, for not getting the
police on horseback properly (which wasn't at all easy), so
I was under some pressure. After fleeing the Nazis, Simon
had worked on *Picture Post*, so he belonged to that tradition
which saw the photographer's moral responsibility as being to
show what was wrong with the world, so that people of good
will would do something about it. Anyway, when I got there
nothing was going on, so we went off to breakfast – only to
find when we came back that all hell had broken loose. The
police had been making repeated charges up the road, but
as always it was a very unequal conflict. Anyway, I picked up
the end of it. Previously the police would have tried to stop
you taking pictures, but this time they seemed to have taken
the decision that they were going to trash the miners in full
view of the cameras. I got knocked over into someone's front
garden, and a woman started calling for an ambulance for an
injured picket. The police charge that had passed us had begun to come back, and there was a police horse right next to
me; what you can't actually see in the famous picture (fig 15),
which is a vertical crop of an image taken with a wide-an gle
lens, is that there's the boot of a mounted police officer right
next to me. Anyway, the officer in the picture shouted: 'I'll
have you as well, you bitch' and he came cantering down and
took a swing at her; if you look closely at the picture you'll
see a miner has grabbed her belt and pulled her back so that
he just missed her.

The picture of Lesley being attacked was published on the
front page of *Labour Weekly*, 22 June 1984. Under the headline
'She was only trying to help ...' it ran the following story:
> Her crime? She was trying to help a picket with crushed
> ribs outside Orgreave coking works. 'I was trying to
> keep out of the way and was stood on the pavement. I

was shouting for someone to call an ambulance for the pickets who had been badly injured. Suddenly this horse came galloping at me and the policeman hurled abuse at me and took a swipe at my head. It was terrifying', said Boulton, a member of Sheffield Women Against Pit Closures. 'The police were completely out of control. They had pushed the pickets right into the village and were just lashing out and hitting anyone who was not wearing a uniform.' John Harris, the photographer who captured this picture, ended up in a bush after he dived away from the mounted police officer, who also took a swing at him. Boulton added: 'It was clear to me from early on in the morning that the police tactics used caused the violence. The pickets had not gone to Orgreave wanting that sort of battle'.

This picture was used very widely in the Left press in Britain and abroad, and also in mainstream overseas publications like the German news magazine *Stern*. It played an extremely important role in both the national and international campaign in support of the striking miners, and indeed rapidly became a modern icon, immediately summing up in one intensely dramatic image the brutality of the state's onslaught on the striking miners and on all those who dared to support them.

'Iconic photographs assume special significance in respect to the past. Iconic images rise above many other images and the vast background of print journalism to shape understanding of specific events and periods, both at the time of their original publication and subsequently … [They] are widely recognized and remembered, are understood to be representations of historically significant events, activate strong emotional identification or response, and are reproduced across a range of media, genres, or topics'. (*No Caption Needed: Iconic Photographs, Public Culture, and Liberal Democracy*, Robert Hariman and John Louis Lucaites, University of Chicago Press, 2007).

Lesley Boulton: I do think the photograph is iconic in the sense that it's about power and the extremes to which the state, and the functionaries of the state, will go to in order to enforce their will on the public. Looking at the image you can see that the state wasn't going to tolerate this sort of dissent. If they had to knock people's heads off they would do so and they didn't care. I personally was shocked by the violence of the police; even though I'd experienced it at Greenham Common, it was much greater during the strike. So yes, it says a lot about what the state will do to shut people up and how the state didn't care about what happened to the miners and to the communities in which they lived. And that's still true to this day.

John Harris: I think the reason why it's become iconic is that it was politically a soft picture, and that quality is intensified by the *Labour Weekly* headline 'She was only trying to help ... ' She wasn't someone who'd been daring to throw bricks at the police and actively resisting. It's a bit like a First World War propaganda picture with the nasty Hun attacking a nun. There was a contemporaneous image which I took, and which was used as a double-page spread by *Stern*, of a miner being thrashed over the bonnet of his car by a riot copper, which was a much harder image. I was surprised that there weren't hundreds of pictures like this all over the place, as this kind of thing was happening all around me. In terms of images of violence, even the Left press was reluctant to print pictures of the miners fighting back, and I had a certain inbuilt bias against taking them, quite honestly. Firstly, on the practical level, you might have got your head kicked in by miners around you, who might have thought you worked for the Right-wing press. But secondly, we didn't think that these were the kinds of images which would get used by the media which supported the miners. So there was a bit of self-censorship going on at times, to be honest. But having said that, what never ceased to amaze me was the extent to which these huge burly miners didn't react; they put up with all sorts of provocation, often at great length and in good humour, before they finally reacted – if at all. A picture like this was acceptable to the people in the Labour Party who were decrying violence by the striking miners, so in my view it became iconic for political reasons; the violence of this police officer was so unacceptable by any standard. But the experience in the pit villages was that this was typical of the way in which the strike was being policed.

So there was a variety of ways in which the picture was seen – as is the case with all images, of course, depending on the context and on how they are used in relation to the dominant narrative. There were separate narratives about what was actually going on in the miners' strike, and the picture was used differently in those different narratives. The issue of violence was central to both the dominant and oppositional narratives of the strike. We were trying to produce pictures which showed where the violence really lay. The mainstream narrative said that it was the miners who were violent (and undemocratic), and this gave the Labour Party and the trade union leadership the excuse not to back them. We were trying to show that the violence was the organised violence of the state.

Pictures can make difference. People often talk about the Vietnam war being lost in the front rooms of America; in fact, of course, it was lost in Vietnam, but because the war was increasingly contested at home, the images of it became hugely significant. So where the dominant narrative is in trouble, photographs can become emblematic and can play an important political and ideological role in changing the world.

However, the mainstream British press at first dealt with the image by ignoring it entirely, with the exception of the *Observer*, 24 June 1984, which printed a small version of it as an accompaniment to an article by Nick Davies headed ' "Police make their own law" in pit war', although the paper 'balanced' it with a picture of an injured policeman. It was not until the Labour MP Jo Richardson produced a copy of the picture at a debate on the policing of the strike at the Labour Party conference on 3 October 1984 that the mainstream press actually acknowledged its existence at all – and then only in order to attempt to trash it. Thus the *Daily Mail*, 3 October, alleged that the IFL, which it helpfully described as 'a co-operative of photographers specializing in trade union work for Left-Wing papers', had 'offered it only to Left-of-Centre newspapers' and that 'other Fleet Street dailies, including the *Daily Mail*, were never told of its existence'. But whilst it is true that the image was offered first to the Left press, there was of course nothing whatsoever to stop other papers applying to the IFL to use it subsequently – as indeed the *Observer* did. The article also quoted the Police Federation as describing the photograph as 'inconclusive', with spokesman Tony Judge adding: 'A picture is two-dimensional and should be treated with great care. If the police officer was as near to her as the photograph suggests, it's hard to see how he missed her'. A similar point was made by the same day's *Telegraph*. Remarkably, this controversy even made its way into the pages of the august *British Journal of Photography*, whose November 1984 issue carried an editorial which referred to a photograph which 'alleged to show a mounted policeman swinging his truncheon towards a woman demonstrator [sic]. The picture was widely circulated as anti-police propaganda and examination of it brings no suspicion of the manipulation which has been suggested. Whether or not the apparent proximity of policeman and demonstrator is an illusion resulting from the foreshortening produced by a long lens is difficult to ascertain and we understand the photographer has denied this. [In fact he was using a wide-angle lens]. The main reason for doubting that the photograph really shows quite what it appears to do is a purely human one. Surely no person being charged by a mounted policeman swinging a truncheon towards her, could possibly maintain the equanimity and freedom from apprehension shown on this woman's face'.

Lesley Boulton: It's hardly surprising that the mainstream press first of all just ignored the picture and then tried to undermine it. After all, the photo was an image of a woman holding a camera, not a brick. If you think about it, what does that mean? A woman in her thirties holding a camera, for God's sake! The media just couldn't explain it. The image didn't fit with their political agenda. So they had to find fault with John and me instead. And it was horrendous, absolutely awful. As a result, I started to receive hate mail. I had two teenage children at the time, and it was very frightening. And it didn't end there. When I initiated legal proceedings in order to press charges for assault, it became very clear that the police weren't just going to roll over. I remember giving a statement at my local police station in Sheffield and the whole thing was very intimidating. I was made to feel that it would be unwise for me to pursue the matter through the courts, so I didn't. The accusation that the photo was somehow montaged was absolutely horrible.

In *1984*, George Orwell wrote: 'If you want a picture of the future, imagine a boot stamping on a human face – forever'. The iconic image of the real 1984 turned out to be not so different – a mounted policeman brutally attacking a defenceless woman who was simply trying to help an injured man. And we would do well to remember that Orwell added: 'The face will always be there to be stamped upon. The heretic, the enemy of society, will always be there, so that he can be defeated and humiliated over again'.

'We are women, we are strong…'
Hilary Wainwright

The shared experience of the extreme circumstances of the miners' strike and of working together in support of the strike produced a profuse and rich literature from women in the mining communities, or women working closely with them. There has been much academic and journalistic writing too, trying to document and understand this inspiring example of the strength of working class women organising in support of both their men and their communities. But with the defeat of the strike and, in many cases the fragmentation and steady disintegration of their communities,[1] a common experience gave way to many individual paths, some converging, many shaped by common values, but not easy to trace or to document.

The women active in the strike made many efforts to continue to work together and even to try and find a common focus for the new kind of politics which many tentatively thought they were creating in action. In many localities they continued to meet. In Easington they did so for five or six years 'to discuss politics and for a natter over a drink' as Heather Wood describes below, Women Against Pit Closures tried to gain what, at the time, they hoped might be some institutional stability by affiliating to the NUM but, while their role during the strike was respected by the men, a permanent partnership once the strike was over was dismissed by a narrow majority of NUM delegates as a step too far. Bonds of friendship and support continued to this day, leading to get-togethers of various sorts at anniversaries and the like. But the complexity and variety of the different histories has clearly daunted all but a small band of intrepid and highly committed researchers. Here I will simply illustrate this complexity with two personal stories and direct readers to the small amount of research which does exist.[2]

The stories are from the same region (County Durham) and from women with very similar values but they confirm the results of thorough research that there was no simple before and after the strike. These differences, and wider, could be multiplied hundreds of times across the coalfields.

Juliana Heron: 'community' councillor

Before the strike Juliana Heron was, in her own words, 'a full-time housewife.' Now, 25 years later, she's Labour mayor of Hetton (having been mayor of Sunderland in 2003-2004). Her husband Bob was a fitter at the local Eppleton pit. Soon after the strike began there was a meeting of women affected by the strike, 'wives, mothers, even grandmothers. It was our future; we had to fight.' From then on she threw herself into the fight for the future of her community.

She thrived in the collective environment of a well-organised network: organising the food for the men and families, being the delegate of the Hetton women's support group to the Durham area, speaking at rallies to win support, representing the Durham women at a miners' holiday 'camp' in East Germany, and more. As she became more aware she extended her reach beyond mining connections, joining up with Greenham Common Women and the Molesworth Peace Camp. 'It was a political awakening,' she remembers. 'Up to then I had voted because women had struggled for the vote. And I'd voted Labour because Labour was instilled in me; I couldn't imagine voting for any other party. But that was the sum of my politics.' It was a personal awakening too: 'My confidence grew. I felt I could make a difference.'

She's matter of fact about the defeat of the strike - though in Eppleton the end was difficult and sad, with many of the men crossing the picket line. 'We were defeated, there's no doubt about it. But we had to carry on. When the pit had gone we had to fight for something else for the town. We had to keep involved.' During the strike, Juliana found that people came to her with their problems and after the strike she turned this capacity for problem-solving into a regular kind of commitment to the community by volunteering for Age Concern and Victim Support. 'Before the strike, I would never have considered volunteering,' she said, 'but after that year of being with people, it was natural.'

From there, the drive to fight for her community led her to become a parish councillor and then a town councillor and then, after her daughter had grown up, to be a city councillor in Sunderland and, eventually, mayor. She lost her seat in the last election but definitely wants to get back. Though formally she's a Labour councillor and loyal to her local party, she defines herself as a 'community' councillor.

She thinks her sense of the Labour Party is specific to the experience of the pit villages in county Durham. The party there is strikingly women dominated. It's as if women have moved in to fill the vacuum left by the collapse of the NUM 'which used to run the party in this area'. There are two kind of women: 'the ones, quite elderly now, who were always doing the backroom work making tea and delivering leaflets but who now have come to the fore; then those of us active in the strike who were willing to do the background work but wanted to have real decision-making power.' Juliana feels the men recognised the role they'd played during the strike and didn't mind them taking that power. But maybe the men didn't have much choice.

The Labour Party and the local authority it controls isn't the only source of power in Hetton. In the decades since the strike, the local residents associations have grown in importance. Last year – 2008 – they won a victory with the local authority: to share power in deciding how government regeneration money will be spent. It's over one million pounds. 'Not enough, mind,' complains Juliana.

It's not only in the public world that Juliana feels that the mining communities are striking back. At the end of our conversation she returns to her family. Her eldest two children are now 40 and late 30s. She reflects on the fact that, in terms of age, they are 'Thatcher's children 'But,' she says proudly, they've not turned out that way. They are not "I'm all right Jack" people. They believe in society.' The strike was their formative experience. She tells of their unselfishness: 'Here were a 12 and 14 year-old refusing Christmas presents so that their 3 year-old sister could enjoy a traditional visit from Father Christmas.'

'Terrible things happened like police men (not the local bobbies) mocking them, waving money at them. There was another side too: having their meals at the miners' welfare, experiencing the solidarity and support.' She described how they'd grown up as politically aware and active adults: 'I think the children from the mining areas have got a completely different perspective.'

Heather Wood: only just recovering

That thought of another generation striking back would cheer up Heather Wood, who was the driving force behind Save Easington Area Mines (SEAM) and the women's support group associated with it, and is a widely respected organiser and thinker in the area. 'If she came to my door,' she told me, talking of Mrs. Thatcher, 'I'd be strong. I'd speak my mind. She'd never know how broken I was. Afterwards though, I'd be exhausted.' Heather was talking about what Thatcher's defeat of the miners' strike had done to her, to her health and to her spirit.

She'd been politically active long before the strike, not so much in the Labour Party as in the community. With foresight, she and her husband and others had set up SEAM a year before the strike. Soon after the strike began, many of the women in Easington District got together: '200 of us met in the council chamber.' It was not the first time women had come together to take action in Easington. Heather was aware of something of a tradition. She even remembers as a child in the 60s how, 'the women poured on to the streets with their prams to occupy the streets and stop the traffic to get baths in the colliery houses.' And they won.

The struggle in 1984-85 was of a different order. Heather felt this harshly - though she has no regrets: 'I gave everything I'd got, and when we lost I felt if we couldn't win then, when could we?' She was exhausted in every way. Totally drained. 'I felt I'd become owned by the public...' She describes visiting her doctor: 'He said that if I was in my coffin in the corner and someone asked me to help them I would say "Yes" and he was probably right.'

It was not just her health that was broken, it was her spirit too. Behind this was a perception that it wasn't just that Thatcher had defeated the miners' strike, it was also that her values, her credo that 'there is no such thing as society' had become a self-fulfilling prophecy. By her defeat of the one social group who had stood up to her she'd succeeded in creating 'a society in which individualism, everyone for themselves, became normal.' For Heather it was the defeat of everything she believed in and held dear.

For someone whose spirit was broken however, and whose health has been declining Heather Wood's life has been remarkable. 'I made myself keep going.' For eight years she was the youngest one of the few women councillors on Durham County Council, with responsibilities for education and social services. She was ' very outspoken which did not go down well at all.' Then in 1993 she got a full-time job as a probation service officer. 'I thought that was the best way I could do something to right the wrongs that had been done to people.' She worked with young offenders, trying to show them that there was another way. 'I was challenging, showing how their behaviour hurt others, but showing them they were not alone; maintaining the punitive side but helping them unravel their predicaments.'

Fifteen years on and after ten years of New Labour, she's had her fill of Thatcherite values mark 2, seeping deep into the way public service were run. 'The probation service was losing its 'caring, social side. It became purely punitive.' The rightward evolution of the Labour Party deepened her depression: 'I was very disillusioned with Labour.'

But the solidarity built up during the strike is still there, especially amongst the women. 'In Easington we continued meeting for 5 or 6 years after the strike to talk politics and natter over a drink. We got together again over the 20th anniversary. We know we are there for each other, even if we don't meet. We are like sisters. We could get together if we're needed.'

She detects a new spirit in herself and in others. Now it's only her health that holds her back. If it wasn't for that she would be out there campaigning. She's proud that community pressure has won an experiment to impose regulations and obligations on unregistered landlords. 'I'd be organising demonstrations, going over the top' to get rid of a derelict school, an eye sore of a listed building which occupies the centre of Easington. 'It means we have a dead centre; it stops us moving on.' Certainly Heather is moving on. And knowing her, she'll find a away of not letting her ill-health get in the way. Maybe her path will converge in some way with Juliana's; they are both fighting for the needs of their communities and showing that there is such a thing as society and remaking it, as the rotten edifices of Thatcherism collapse.

Interweaving the personal and the political
Both these women, in very different ways, either began and maintained (Juliana) or continued in a profoundly altered way (Heather) a relationship to both party and community politics. But research also shows that some women moved

from public and political concerns to pick up the threads of their disrupted private and family lives – going 'back to normal' they described it.[3] Other research, borne out in a complex ways by these two stories, points to ways in which the strong community networks developed or built on to give support to the strike were, by the turn of the century more likely to be the basis of welfare support than political action.[4] These personal stories point to how strong political (with a small 'p') values underlay both voluntary and paid welfare work - Juliana's engagement in Age Concern and Victim Support and Heather's decision to become a probation service officer.

The work of Jean Spence and Carol Stevenson is particularly interesting because it is part of a long term personal and political engagement with Women Against Pit Closures.[5] The main conclusion which they draw from the discussion at this conference and from other research over a long period concerns what they describe as 'the interweaving of personal and political concerns'. This, they argue, frequently predates the strike, 'was effectively mobilised in its support and continues afterwards. The strike affirmed and gave concrete expression to these women's beliefs, but it did not create them. These categories within a continuing pattern of activism illustrate firstly the significance of commitment to an ideal or set of principles - whether to 'community' or to a political philosophy, in provoking the activism of some women during the strike. Those motivated in this manner have been most likely to remain active in the long term'. Secondly, they imply that for most of these women, the strike did not rupture their life and set them on an entirely different path: 'For the majority the strike enhanced their political awareness and presented them with opportunities which had previously seemed out of reach, but it did so in a context which was usually prefigured by pre-strike interests, identities and desires'.

Behind this is a criticism of dualities of personal/political, public/private, home/work. For Jean Spence and Carol Stevenson these dichotomies, often used in discussions of the experience of women's roles during and after the strike, obscure the emotional and personal dimensions of the ways of organising that these women created and which kept them going and maintained strong bonds, if not political organization, after the strike.

Certainly the interweaving of the personal and political is one common thread of the stories of Juliana Heron and Heather Wood. It is maybe one reason why it's so common to find women being involved in voluntary work in the years since the strike. In these interviews they talked about it in quite collective and transformative ways, and imbued it with social and broadly political values.

A challenge for the future of the left
One of the challenges which the experience of the women in the mining. or now ex-mining communities, both during and after the strike present to the left is how to develop a way of organising built on this close interaction between finding solutions to the problems of daily social life on the one hand, and wider political change on the other. In a sense this fusion was the radical core of the early trade union movement. It got lost in the division between the industrial and political wings of the labour movement in the formation and institutional framework of the Labour Party in 1906. The women's movement around the strike brought it together again under very extreme circumstances. The detailed history of the scattered legacy of that experience, building on the research so far, would contain many insights for a realistic strategy for a lasting fusion of these two essential dimensions of social change.

Notes

1   See *Capital and Class* Special Issue on the miners' strike (no 87 Autumn 2005) for several useful bibliographies

2   Jean Spence and Carol Stephenson, *Female Involvement in the Miners' Strike 1984-85* (2007); Meg Allen, 'Trajectories of Activism', Sociological Research Online. Volume 12,.Issue 1 (2000); M.P Shaw, *Carrying on the Strike: The Politics of Women Against Pit Closures into the 1990s.* Ph D Thesis, University of Manchester (1993); Durham.T Strangleman, *Women in Protest and Beyond: Greenham Common and Mining Support Groups.* PhD Thesis University of Manchester (2001); 'Networks, Place and Identities in Post-Industrial Mining Communities', *International Journal of Urban and Regional Research, 25* (2) June pp253 -267; D. Waddington, *Out of the Ashes? The social impact of industrial contraction and regeneration on Britain's Mining Communities.* Routledge (2001)

3   Shaw (1993)

4   Strangleman (2001)

5   An important moment in their research, and in the recent history of Women Against Pit Closures, was a conference in the North East, marking the twentieth anniversary of the strike at which around 20 women activists came together 'to create a forum of discussion about the issues most important to them, and to decide whether there were grounds to reunite twenty years on'. Its report is available through a special edition of *Capital and Class* in Autumn 2005. Edited by Anne Suddick, who wrote a very comprehensive editorial: 'The past we inherit; the future we build'.

The after-memory: documentary films and the aftermath of the miners' strike
Patricia Holland

There is a dramatic moment in the film of *Billy Elliott* where Billy's father takes the unthinkable step of going back to work to help young Billy leave his strike-bound village for ballet school in London. His older son, active in the strike, is distraught, but the options are stark. Billy's special talent may be rewarded – the posters for the stage version picture his exuberant leap out of his northern childhood to metropolitan success – but without the solidarity of the strike, the community he leaves behind will certainly collapse. This is the tragedy of a show billed as a 'feel good' experience – the tragedy of an enforced opposition between individual and community. It was a theme bleakly echoed by Dave Nixon, an ex-miner featured in the BBC2 documentary *The Miners' Strike* (2004), 'Thatcher succeeded. It's all individualism now. It's "I don't give a damn about you. Why should I?" '

The film of *Billy Elliott* was released in 2000. It was a great success, and the stage musical has, at the time of writing, been playing for three years in London to full houses. Together with *Brassed Off* (1996) and the even more successful *Full Monty* (1997) it created something of a genre. These fictions set the collapse of heavy industry against personal success in the leisure industries – music, entertainment and high culture. The old virtues of masculine solidarity through physical labour are seen as giving way to ambiguous sexualities and the pleasures of performance. Such highly contemporary themes clearly ring a bell with audiences – and they made for optimistic narratives. But the documentary work which has dealt with the aftermath of the strike was forced to come to grips with far more disturbing parts of the story. Programmes made around the twentieth anniversary of the strike explored a legacy of bitterness and social collapse against a background where even the physical remnants of the mining industry were being erased.

In 1983, photographer John Davies was commissioned by Amber, the film and photography collective based in the North East, to document the working landscapes of the Durham coalfield, from pit heads and slag heaps to railway sidings and industrial buildings. In 2004, as part of Amber's *Coal Field Stories* project, he revisited the sites of his earlier pictures. The paired images show a striking erosion of the visible signs of industry. Empty fields and car parks have replaced the clutter of working mines and factories. A sequence of desolate aerial shots in the ITV documentary, *Children of the Miners' Strike* (2004), makes a similar point. Twenty years later, for the communities which had depended on the mines, this active erasure continued to pose questions about the terms of their own survival.

Since the 1970s Amber have been close to the communities they represented in their work. Their three films on mining communities at the turn of the 21st century use both drama and documentary. *It's the Pits* (1994), *The Scar* (1997) and *Like Father* (2001) focus in turn on the experiences of young people, women and men. But the originality and commitment of Amber's work has meant that it has not been widely seen. By contrast I want to look at the ways in which mainstream television has, in its various ways, reflected on the strike and its significance. Documentaries on the BBC, ITV and Channel Four have dealt not only with the events themselves and their political and economic context, but also with the different interpretations of that history. They show an awareness of the cultural representations and mythologies which have given coal and coal miners a particular place in the national consciousness and have reflected on the ways in which that place was transformed in the 1980s. Such reconstructions of memory and the active shifting of established values are what I have described as the 'after-memory'.

Strike: When Britain Went to War (2004) sets out to demonstrate incompatible political systems and changing attitudes. 1984, as well as being the date of George Orwell's nightmare vision of a totalitarian state, was the year Jayne Torvill and Christopher Dean won the winter Olympics with their superb performance of Ravel's Bolero. Does this cultural landmark pinpoint the mood of the 1980s more than the miners' strike? asks the film. Was popular politics now to be celebrity based, like Bob Geldof's Band Aid, rather than class based? The radical political and economic shifts of the 1980s were creating an equally potent cultural shift, which had the effect of devaluing the miners' cause and the image of what miners and coal mining stood for. The events of the strike are traced through interviews and news footage, but threaded through the film is the music and entertainment of the era. Torvill and Dean are juxtaposed with the irresponsible anarchy of *The Young Ones*, the music of Wham and advertisements for the sell-off of British Telecom. The film ends with champagne-swilling city workers and that iconic creation of the 1980s, Harry Enfield as 'Loadsamoney' – track-suited, working class and flaunting his wad of £50 notes.

As the film makes clear, the strike was solidly supported by students, intellectuals and the left as well as the trade union working class. But Phil Woolas (at the time a student leader, now a Labour MP and Home Office minister) argues, 'the non-trade union working class... wanted this new economy. They wanted this privatised, share-owning democracy'. In the triumphalist words of Thatcher adviser and public relations specialist, Tim Bell, 'the miners' strike has absolutely changed the way we live in our society..[it] is the seminal moment in which the left lost and the right won'. The conflicting frameworks are dramatically clear. 'We were fighting to save villages and pits' says Arthur Jackson, a striking miner from

Nottingham, 'I can't see how anybody can lose that sort of argument'. But for the rabid right-wing editor of *The Sun*, Kelvin McKenzie, a miners' victory 'would send Britain back into the dark ages'.

The language of war, battle and violence echoes through the programmes. *Strike* makes much of the intransigence of the opposing leaders, Arthur Scargill and Margaret Thatcher. 'It was a titanic struggle between two armies' declares the commentary. *The Miners' Strike* was trailed as re-living 'the pumping adrenalin, searing emotions, violence and hatred...in the deep and bitter dispute.' Instead of Torvill and Dean, this film was framed by a group of ex-miners from the Yorkshire village of Hatfield. Its thumping music, reconstructions and dramatic visuals – big close ups, textured shots, angles and impressionistic editing – positively wallowed in the physical attacks between police and pickets, and between striking and working miners. 'We were taught how to hate' says Dave Nixon, 'of all the things they did to us, that was probably the worst'.

Scrutinising the political record and re-visiting the details of such a pivotal event, as well as reviewing the perspective of various participants and commentators, are all important functions of documentary programming. But, in many ways, films which show the long, slow aftermath of the strike can be even more telling. Rather than adrenalin pumping, headline-grabbing conflict, this group of documentaries reveals much longer and deeper struggles. These films visit the second and third generations in the mining villages, and lay out in painful detail how the destruction of the industry is reverberating down the generations.

A *Billy Elliott* of 2004 might end up like Gary of *Children of the Miners' Strike* (BBC 2004) whose mother is engaging in a heroic struggle to keep him off heroin; or like Darren of *Wasted* (C4 2002), a school boy who felt he had nothing to look forward to. His family had been miners for five generations, but his 35-year-old father, Stephen, had not worked for nine years. Stephen spent his time with his racing pigeons and cherished a vain hope that they would win him a big prize.

Children of the Miners' Strike begins with newsreel footage of picket-line confrontations while introducing a generation that has turned to drugs. 'In the pit villages they used to say that coal ran in their blood' says the commentary, 'twenty years later it's heroin'. 'I've been all over the world' says Buzz, a night shelter worker. 'I came back about ten years ago, and walked into my village and there was just smackheads in a row...I'm not in New York, I'm not in the middle of London, I'm in my own fucking village....' The hero of the film is Donna, who works in the shelter for homeless addicts, and who time and again gives her 22-year old son Gary another chance. But he steals her money, disappears without warning and breaks every promise, despite prison sentences and numerous rehabilitation efforts. The heroic masculinity of the *Battle of Orgreave* and *The Miners' Strike* has shifted to a less spectacular heroism, that of sheer survival, sustained, against all the odds, by strong women. Documentaries like these do not re-view the past, but are lived, painfully, in the here and now. We agonise with Donna as Gary is found with a needle yet again; we join in Stephen's desperate wait for his pigeons to come home.

These films which deal with the aftermath of the strike carry a poignant after-memory of coal mining and its special place in British national narratives. 'Mining communities have always struggled, have always had to face disaster' says Donna, 'it's true life and the grit of life'. 'We had previously been called the salt of the earth' says miner Mick Mulligan bitterly in *The Miners' Strike* ' it was a bit dirty of [Thatcher] to call us the enemy within'. The mythology of the miner, as 'the noblest expression of the British working classes' a 'working class legend' with 'an emotional pull on the Left', draws scorn from the anti-strike commentators in Channel Four's *Strike*.

The traditional image of the coal miner with his pick and lamp is familiar from the earliest days of cinema. A day in the life of a coal miner was filmed in Wigan in 1910, while the classic, *Coalface* (1935), was at the cutting edge of avant-garde modernity, with its poetry, chanting, choral singing and a-tonal music written by the young Benjamin Britten. But this 'working class legend' was underpinned by respect and by a recognition of the necessity of such dangerous work. 'Coal mining is the basic industry of Britain' declares the opening commentary. Hovering between myth-making and painful reality, the film points to the misery that has been the cost of prosperity. 'Every working day four miners are killed and over 450 injured and maimed. Every year in Great Britain, one in every five miners is injured'. The avant-garde style does not seem inappropriate for this contemplation of the contradictions of modernity and progress. With the Second World War came morale-boosting films which recognised miners as an essential part of the war effort. The injuries sustained by Goronwy, the miner in Humphrey Jennings's *Diary for Timothy* (1946), were as serious as those sustained by Peter the pilot, shot down by enemy fire.

But by the 1980s coal was no longer 'the basic industry' and coal mining was no longer essential to the nation's survival. The economic reality which had underpinned the mythology has been drained away. The myth could now be dismissed as mere romanticism, an 'emotional pull'. Films about the aftermath of the strike came burdened with this loss of respect, this changing after-memory.

However, by the 2000s there was a new set of buzz-words: 'community', 'participation' and, above all, 're-generation'. A Channel Four series followed the Castleford Project, in which English Partnerships (the 'National Regeneration Agency'), together with the Coalfields Regeneration Trust and local district councils, set about 'renewing' what had been a thriving Yorkshire mining town, decimated by the closure of its pits. *Kevin McCloud and the Big Town Plan* (2008) is not designed to reflect on the 1984 strike, but has an extraordinary resonance when viewed against that history. The Castleford project had a double aim, to improve the area on behalf of those who live there – and there was extensive consultation and participation – and to 'regenerate' it, in order to attract new investment and new housing.

The edition of 18 August 2008 focussed on parks, 'that great Victorian invention that consolidated civic pride and was a meeting place for people, for everybody -for society,' says McCloud, adding 'until Margaret Thatcher declared there was 'no such thing as society'.' The programme follows three projects over a number of years, beginning with the earliest discussions and reviewing their use three years after completion. Two were undertaken in liaison with community activists who helped choose the architects and had an input into the design. Three years later, both of these parks were busy and active, filled with local children clambering over the adventure equipment. Once more the hero of the story was a local woman, Rita Davidson. For Rita, when the mines closed down followed by other local industries, people felt useless. 'Life's not worth living, you just go deeper into depression… the Community Group has got me out of this'.

The third project was based in the tiny village of New Fryston, where only 70 homes were left after houses and the school were demolished along with the pit. Here a prestigious sculpture park was designed by prize winning American architect, Martha Schwartz, chosen, this time without consultation, by English Partnerships and given a million pounds to spend. Schwartz sees herself as a visionary, an artist. For her 'artists are supposed to visualise a new world'. She is clearly bemused by any notion of local involvement and serving local needs. 'The world won't leave them alone,' she declares of the uncooperative residents, 'change is going to happen. It's coming. They must change'. Her re-designed 'village green' literally faced away from the existing community, towards a putative new community which, it was said, would be attracted to the site. This was the scheme opened by the Castleford MP and Housing Minister, Yvette Cooper, while the locals looked on with scepticism. The signs of the industry and its history had here been most effectively eroded.

Films mentioned
Billy Elliott (2000)
Director: Stephen Daldry, Script Lee Hall
Working Title
Brassed Off (1996)
Director: Mark Herman
Children of the Miners' Strike (2004)
Producer/Director: Jess Fowle
True North Productions for ITV's Real Life Series
Coalface (1935)
Producer John Grierson
EMPO
A Day in the Life of a Coal Miner (1910)
Kineto
A Diary for Timothy (1946)
Director: Humphrey Jennings
Crown Film Unit
The Full Monty
Director: Peter Cattaneo
It's the Pits (1994)
Amber Films
Kevin McCloud and the Big Town Plan (Channel 4 2008)
Talkback Production
Like Father (2001)
Amber Films

The Miners' Strike (BBC2 2004)
Producer/Director: Steven Condie
The Scar (1997)
Amber Films
Strike: When Britain Went to War (C4 2004)
Producer Janice Sutherland Director: Kate Werran
Blakeway Productions
Wasted (C4 2002)
Producer/Director: Pamela Gordon
October Films

Unfinished business: demythologising the battle of Orgreave[1]
Michael Bailey

Shortly after the 1984/85 miners' strike had come to an end, the socialist historian Raphael Samuel noted that the meaning of the strike would be determined not 'by the terms of settlement...or even by the events of the past year but by the way in which it is assimilated in popular memory, by...retrospective understanding both in the pit villages themselves and in the country at large'.[2] Following Samuel's example, I mean to demonstrate that the legacy of miners' strike is still an ideological battle, in which competing cultural representations continue to shape the public's understanding of an event that, even now, resonates in parts of the nation's collective consciousness as 'living history'.[3] More than this, I want to argue that although the strike was a catastrophic defeat – not just for miners, but the communities in which they lived and trade unionism – it is imperative that the Left maintain the struggle in and through the potential creation of new representations that seek to democratise the mediation of the strike, by making visible the lived experiences of former pickets and their families. That is to say, mediations that critically challenge – or demythologise – the way in which the miners were dehumanised and the strike discredited. Not only because such texts hold out the promise of raising public awareness of what actually happened twenty-five years ago. Or that they provide affirmation for those miners and families most affected by the strike-action, the subsequent closure of pits and the gradual demise of whole communities, important though this is. But because they also remind working people, and the labour movement generally, of the lessons learnt and that the more general issues surrounding the strike remain a site of political struggle in the present instant.

Though there are various cultural forms that fulfil the above criteria (for example, *The Miners' Tapes*, Ken Loach's *Which Side Are You On?*, Chris Curling's *The Last Pit in the Rhondda*, Mark Herman's *Brassed-Off*, Stephen Daldry's *Billy Elliot*, Peter Flannery's *Our Friends in the North*, William Ivory's *Faith*, Frank and Allan Brammah's *Margarella*, *The Moles and the Money Tree*, David Peace's *GB84*, Mark Hudson's *Coming Back Brockens*, an array of popular songs, not to mention the numerous written and photo-documentary accounts of the strike produced by miners and miners' wives) I want to concentrate on a collaborative artistic project that involved the partial re-enactment of the infamous confrontation between the police and striking miners at the British Steel coking plant at Orgreave near Sheffield. The event was conceived by the artist Jeremy Deller, already known for his pioneering of 'Acid Brass' in the late 1990s, and produced by Artangel, an alternative art initiative that commissions innovative contemporary art projects across a variety of media.[4] As well as it being a live event, the reconstruction was filmed by Mike Figgis and subsequently broadcast by Channel Four in 2002.[5] Furthermore, though many of the participants were members of battle re-enactment societies, a significant number of the project's subjects were veterans of the original conflict, that is ex-miners playing themselves. Above all, both the reconstruction and documentary were conceived as a political spectacle that would commemorate an event –the strike as a whole– that remains one of the most bitter and protracted industrial disputes in British history. And of all the incidents that took place during the strike, the so-called 'battle of Orgreave' was one of the most violent and bloodiest, culminating on the 18 June 1984 when almost 5,000 pickets confronted approximately the same number of policemen.[6] The rest, as they say, is history. Or is it?

Whilst the perception at the time, and it is one that still

endures to this day, was that Orgreave was a decisive turning point in the strike, it is important to note that there was nothing guaranteed about the government's defeat of the coal dispute, even in the aftermath of Orgreave. Contrary to state propaganda circulated at the time, subsequent interviews with government and police officials reveal that the strike was a closely fought dispute, and the government was close to backing down on a number of occasions, not least during Orgreave. What is more, the strike has since taken on a life of its own within many former mining communities, one that is not necessarily as defeatist as we might think it is. Though blighted by high levels of unemployment, poverty and anti-social crime, lots of post-industrial mining communities have started to rethink the strike as cultural heritage, in an effort to regenerate the localities in which they live. By re-conceptualising the strike in this way, it has been possible for such communities to secure national and regional funding with which to organise social networks and events, thus enabling them to revalue their collective identity in and through the recovery of 'community memory'. As well as 'giving meaning back to their lives' of the veterans of the strike, such activities also provide an occasion for commemorating both the strike and a whole way of working-class life.[7]

It is with the this kind of optimism in mind that I want to turn my attention to the Deller/Artangel/Figgis collaboration as an exemplar of a cultural text that provides an opportunity to re-evaluate the strike; however, not just an historical event, that is as something lost to history, much less as 'a nightmare on the brain of the living', but as an on-going historical process, as unfinished business.[8]

In terms of the motifs that run throughout *The Battle of Orgreave*, foremost is the brutality of the policing strategy on the day itself and throughout the coal dispute generally. As well as seeing re-enactments we also hear verbal testimony from a variety of people who were veterans of the original conflict – ex-miners, an NUM delegate, a miner's wife – of the police giving chase on foot and on horseback, the use of excessive force, unlawful arrests, draconian curfews, etc. The testimonies are all the more powerful for the fact that among them is a former police officer – who also happened to be a miner – who confirms that, in the run up to the strike, police officers were trained in tactics and policing formations that were then unusual, leading him to comment that the police were preparing themselves for 'a specific role'. Of course, we now know this to be true. And Orgreave was no exception: it epitomised the way in which the police had planned for the strike with military-like precision; indeed, at the 1985 trial of ninety-five Orgreave pickets – all were acquitted – the police officer in charge of Orgreave, Assistant Chief Constable Anthony Clement, openly confessed that the conflict at Orgreave had more or less been orchestrated by the police.[9]

Nor were policing tactics confined to striking miners: whole mining communities were forced to live in what can only be described as a de facto police state. Indeed, the documentary serves as a reminder that the strike became an occasion for the then newly emerging forces of neo-liberalism, not just to defeat the NUM and to settle old scores, but to suppress a particular way of life known to generations of mining families up and down the country. Bearing this in mind, it is hardly surprising that we should witness some of the re-enactors express a heartfelt animosity towards the police on camera. An example of this is when we witness three bemused ex-miners wearing police uniforms and looking deeply uncomfortable after they have been asked to re-enact the part of police officers. Though one of the miners comments on how it might be interesting to see 'the other side of the spectrum', the other two are less sure: one comments on how he's 'not use to owt like this' and how 'he feels a pillock', whilst the other miner simply says that it 'goes against the grain'. What we see is not so much a re-enactment as it is a living, breathing 'structure of feeling' that still differentiates between 'us' and 'them', lest we forget that the threat of coercion – via the police and the armed forces under control of the state – remains a reality in most Western democracies .

Yet another theme, though more implicit than it is explicit, is the contradictory consciousness that many working-class people experienced at the time of the strike. Probably the best example of this is a scene in which we see the former-miner-turned-policeman, clearly upset and remorseful about his part in the strike, telling us how he joined the police because he wanted to do something for the community in which he lived. But thanks to Margaret Thatcher, what he did in fact was to 'help destroy' that community. Though one might not necessarily sympathise with what is, essentially, a secular act of contrition, what this testimony nevertheless illustrates is the way in which the working class were, as noted by Paul Ward, 'pulled in different directions by historical forces'.[10]

Similarly, we see Dave Douglass, an NUM branch delegate at the time, lament the lack of support among the wider labour movement. Even though many workers realised the strike was an attack, not just upon miners, but trade unionism and the working class generally, they refused to get behind the miners as they had done in previous strikes. The fact that the Trades Union Congress and much of the Labour parliamentary party would not openly support the miners, thereby providing the necessary political leadership, undoubtedly exasperated this double consciousness. Indeed, we see only the one politician – the solitary figure of Tony Benn – bearing witness to the atrocities of the strike, which is itself testimony to what can only be described as a miserable level of support among the country's political elite both during and after the strike. In fact, Deller comments on how New Labour would be 'almost embarrassed by talk of the miners' strike because their reaction would be very similar to Margaret Thatcher's government'.

Likewise, an ex-miner notes the continuing closure of mines and the lack of political opposition, an indisputable fact that politicians and the wider trade union movement will one day have to explain, especially now that Britain's energy policy –not least its dependency on foreign imports of oil, gas and coal– is seriously in question.[11]

Of all the events surrounding Orgreave, one of the most controversial was the way in which much of the media coverage at the time was completely lacking in objectivity and impartiality. The most notorious instance of media bias was the BBC's misreporting of the confrontation. Contrary to popular myth, subsequent police video evidence and news coverage from ITN clearly demonstrate that the BBC had misrepresented the skirmish by misleadingly portraying the miners as the aggressors.[12] That a public service broadcaster as revered as the BBC should commit such a dreadful error of editorial judgement still rankles and continues to haunt the corridors of Broadcasting House to this day. More crucially, and as pointed out by Len Masterman at the time, the BBC footage became a convenient 'short-hand reference to picket violence', reinforcing Margaret Thatcher's depiction of the miners as the 'enemy within'.[13] The Battle of Orgreave redresses this misrepresentation, not just by informing us through the oppositional testimony of Tony Benn, who quite rightly states that whoever had taken the decision to re-order the BBC footage 'destroyed the truth of what they reported', but also through Mike Figgis's ironic re-enactment of 'picket violence', done in such a way so as to expose the myth of what we are seeing by deliberately drawing our attention to the subjective and reflexive nature of the documentary itself.[14]

Elsewhere we see the documenting of other commonplace misrepresentations, interestingly, in and through the words and actions of the professional re-enactors. For example, in one scene we see a re-enactor stuntman instructing the extras to fall to the ground upon contact with police shields, followed by a comment that 'there wasn't much baton use on the day in the field', to which he is told by someone out of view of the camera, an ex-miner presumably, to 'behave' and 'what about later on the road'. The re-enactor then admits that this will 'be a bit more brutal'. In another part of the documentary we see Howard Giles, the person in charge of directing the re-enactment and former director of English Heritage's event programme, insisting that each group of miners only be allowed one official stone thrower during the re-enactment, moreover, the thrower must be a practised re-enactor. The miners are then told that if things get out of hand the re-enactment will be stopped and that anybody who does gets out of hand 'won't get paid'. We then see one of the re-enactors – a well spoken person dressed as a policeman – telling the camera that him and his colleagues 'have a few concerns about some of the extras' because they 'don't know when enough's enough'. The camera then cuts to an ex-miner telling his former comrades – a term of reference he uses himself – that the rehearsal so far has just been a play, and that the actual re-enactment is for real, to which another former-miner replies, 'fuck the £160 quid, we're going for it. If they throw us off, they throw us off'. Whilst much of this is said in jest, what these scenes – and others like them – reveal is a genuine anxiety about the likelihood of another violent confrontation; what we witness is an enactment of an actual fear of there being real violence. And the miners are the likely culprits, just as they were twenty-five years ago. Hence, time and time again, we see the extras, mostly ex-miners, subject to an array of rules and occasional threats in case the re-enactment give way to 'the rule of the mob'.

However, as with Figgis's ironic re-telling of the BBC controversy, what the documentary does is to expose the 'what-goes-without-saying' of Orgreave, not least the miners' propensity for violent conduct.[15] Not unlike Bertolt Brecht's Verfremdungseffekt, Figgis uses similar techniques for 'alienation effect', causing the viewing public to critically question what they are seeing and their hitherto assumptions about the culpability of the miners for the violence at Orgreave. As with epic theatre, rather than simply reproduce the myths that dominated public discourse during the dispute, The *Battle of Orgreave* reveals them for what they are.[16] By virtue of its disruptive gesture, that is by enacting many of the aforementioned myths as they are played out in the present, and by juxtaposing these enactments alongside contradictory testimonies and re-enactments, the documentary speaks the myth of the miners' strike. In so doing, it provides the public with a counter-myth, one that demythologises much of the media bias and consequent false consciousness that prevailed at the time. It also reinvigorates and repoliticises the strike for present and future generations of socialists and working people. Though the mines and miners have greatly declined in numbers, the *Battle of Orgreave* reminds us that 'the 84/85 struggle isn't a closed book...the working class are still here...and that the kind of confrontation we witnessed over twenty years ago will arise again in the near future'. Contrary to the prevailing orthodoxy of neo-liberalism, and in spite of the wider political losses endured since the miners' strike, the spectre of a socialist politics continues to haunt society and the miners' strike is very much a part of this historical materialist process, hence the importance that socialists, to paraphrase Walter Benjamin, take 'control of that memory', particularly 'as it flashes in a moment of danger'. In short, the miners' strike –as with all political struggles of the past– may yet 'blast open the continuum of history'.[17]

Notes

1 The idea for this title was partly inspired by a collection of social-realist photographs taken by Phil McHugh, entitled, *Unfinished Business: Photo-text Constructions From The Miners' Strike 1984-5*, London: Coppice Press, 1985.

2   Raphael Samuel, Barbara Bloomfield & Guy Boanas, *The Enemy Within: Pit Villages and the Miners' Strike of 1984-5*, London: Routledge & Kegan Paul Ltd, 1986, p ix.

3   This is all the more salient in light of recent evidence which would suggest that hostilities towards the miners and the mining industry continued well into the 1990s; see Seumas Milne *The Enemy Within: the Secret War Against the Miners*, London & New York: Verso, 1994 for a riveting exposé of the state's continuing efforts to annihilate what little was left of the coal industry and to politically manipulate the strike's legacy, particularly the reputation of the then National Union of Mineworkers' president, Arthur Scargill.

4   Deller also published a book called *The English Civil War Part II*, London: Artangel Press 2002, that documents both the re-enactment and the way in which the event was represented at the time.

5   DVD released by Artangel in 2006, entitled, *A Mike Figgis Film of Jeremy Deller's The Battle of Orgreave.*

6   Prior to this, the ugliest confrontations had been, not surprisingly, in and around the Nottinghamshire coal field. However, a couple of months into the strike, attention turned to the coking plant at Orgreave. The significance of this shift in strategy was twofold: first, Orgreave was the main supply of good quality coking coal needed to power the steel works in Scunthorpe; second, Orgreave was quite literally on the NUM's back doorstep, no more than a fifteen minutes drive from its former headquarters in Sheffield.

7   Carol Stephenson & David Wray, 'Emotional Regeneration Through Community Action in Post-Industrial Mining Communities: The New Herrington Miners' Banner Partnership', in *Capital & Class*, No.87, 2005, pp 175-99. Among the many other analyses of the aftermath of the 1985/85 miners' strike, see David Waddington, Chas Critcher, Bella Dicks & Dave Parry, *Out of the Ashes? The Social Impact of Industrial Contraction and Regeneration on Britain's Mining Communities*, Norwich: The Stationery

Office 2001, David Waddington, Maggie Wykes & Chas Critcher, *Split at The Seams: Community, Continuity and Change after the 1984-5 Coal Dispute*, Milton Keyes: Open University Press 1991. There are also a handful of televisual documentaries that critically investigate the socio-economic consequences of the strike; see, for example, *Real life: Children of the Miner's Strike*. ITV, 2004.

8   See Mark Neocleous, 'Let the Dead Bury Their Dead: Marxism and the Politics of Redemption', *Radical Philosophy 128*, 2004, pp23-32.

9   It should be noted that not only did the trial collapse, moreover, in 1991 South Yorkshire police agreed to pay a £425,000 settlement to thirty-nine miners who sued for assault and wrongful arrest in connection with Orgreave; see Milne *The Enemy Within*, pp 24, and 371-2.

10   Paul Ward, *Documentary: the Margins of Reality*, London & New York: Wallflower, 2005, pp51-2.

11   For a fuller analysis of Britain's failing energy policy, see the special TUC edition of *The Miner*, September 2008, http://www.num.org.uk/?p=publications.

12   See David Jones, Julian Petley, Mike Power & Lesley Wood, *Media Hits the Pits*, London: The Campaign for Press and Broadcasting Freedom 1985.

13   Len Masterman, *Television Mythologies: Stars, Shows and Signs*, London: Comedia, 1984.

14   See Paul Ward, *Documentary*, pp56-7.

15   See Roland Barthes, *Mythologies*, London: Vintage, 1993, pp109-59.

16   See Walter Benjamin, *Understanding Brecht*, London & New York: Verso, 1998, pp1-25.

17   Walter Benjamin, 'On the Concept of History' (Thesis VI) in Harry Zohn (trans.), Howard Eiland & Michael W. Jennings (eds.), *Selected Writings, Vol. 4: 1938-1940*, Cambridge MA: Harvard University Press, 2003, p391; Neocleous, *'Let the Dead Bury Their Dead'*, p30.

Acknowledgments: I am grateful to Dave Waddington and Julian Petley for loaning me valuable primary and secondary source materials that directly relate to the history of the strike and Orgreave in particular.

If only...
Nicholas Jones

When Arthur Scargill visited the Camp for Climate Change
erected outside the Kingsnorth coal-fired power station in
Kent in August 2008, he found himself at odds with a group
of activists who back in the 1980s might well have joined him
in challenging the policies of Margaret Thatcher. Undaunted
by the placards of environmental campaigners declaring 'No
new coal', he used his guest appearance as honorary president
of the National Union of Mineworkers to mount a valiant
defence of the need for a new and integrated energy policy
based on coal and renewables which he hoped would result
in the closure of all nuclear power stations. Delighted though
they were both by the publicity which Scargill attracted and
his criticism of the stop-and-search powers being exercised
by riot police around the camp, the protestors seemed in no
mood to be swayed by what smacked of special pleading by
the NUM and they were adamant that if there was to be any
real chance of reducing greenhouse gas emissions, there had
to be a ban on any future investment in coal-fired generation.
Nonetheless Scargill was as ambitious as ever in presenting
an action plan to revive the coal industry:
— closed pits should be re-opened.
— coal production should be increased to 250 million
tons a year (more than twice the level of the pre 1984
level out of output).
— approval should be given for the construction of a
new generation of coal-fired power stations designed to
incorporate the latest carbon capture technology.
Scargill had every reason to feel emboldened. Opinion
remained divided over whether nuclear power was a safe way
to fight global warming and despite a considerable expansion
in wind farms and other renewable sources of energy, coal

continued to generate 36 per cent of the United Kingdom's electricity and was well placed for a comeback if trials of carbon capture technology proved successful. Kingsnorth had become a target for Greenpeace and a wide cross section of environmentalists after it was selected by the German-owned power company E.ON as the site for a new £1 billion coal-fired station, a planning application which in the summer of 2008 appeared to have the support of the then Secretary of State for Business, John Hutton. Other privatised power generators were also in the process of considering applications for new coal stations at Tilbury in Essex, Blyth in Northumberland and Longannet in Fife.

In view of the strength of unity among protestors at the climate camp and the importance they attached to targeting coal burning as a way reducing global warming, Scargill deserved to be congratulated for entering potentially hostile territory and for arguing the miners' case in his usual forthright manner. Support for carbon capture - not just for coal but also for gas and oil fired power stations - was held up as proof of the NUM's green credentials, an innovation which he said the union had been urging for years through his chairmanship of Energy 2000. He condemned the government's failure to champion clean coal: the lack of investment in technology to remove CO_2 emissions was all the more regrettable bearing in mind that Britain had 'over 1,000 years of coal reserves'.

But Scargill's strident advocacy of a green future for coal could not hide the fact that the NUM was playing catch up. The pioneering work which Britain had done in the development of clean coal technology was one of the many casualties of the 1984-5 strike when sadly the NUM forfeited the leading role it had previously played. Not only had the union lost the leverage it once had over government policy, but its contribution to the wider debate on protecting the environment had largely gone by default.

Early on in my stint as labour correspondent for BBC radio news I had a valuable insight into how it might have been possible for Britain to have taken a commanding lead in technological developments like the capture of CO_2 emissions if only the coal industry and power stations had remained in public ownership and if it had been possible to maintain a fruitful partnership between unions and management. Long-term investment in new pits and equipment had previously kept Britain at the forefront of technological developments in deep mining and, given the chance, I am sure that tackling the pollution caused by burning coal could and would have been given an equally high priority if there been government support and a continued joint commitment towards safeguarding the industry's future.

Having witnessed the optimism of the early 1980s and the faith there was then in coal as a long-lasting energy source for Britain, I have often wondered over the intervening years how the industry might have fared if there had been a negotiated settlement to the 1984-5 strike and if the coalfields had not become a victim of political vengeance and short term commercial expediency. 'If only...' was the working title for a programme which I devised in 2004 to mark the 20th anniversary of the strike but which, to my disappointment, failed to attract the interest of either radio or television commissioning editors.

I accept that once the fight against pit closures and job losses took precedence over all other activity, both in the run-up to the strike and during its devastating aftermath, there was no time for the forward thinking which had taken place under Scargill's predecessor Joe Gormley, who as NUM President had established a close working relationship with Sir Derek Ezra, the then chairman of the National Coal Board. The two men were united in their desire to develop new and more efficient uses of coal and they exploited to the full the collaborative ethos which a well-run nationalised industry could engender to extract maximum financial support from the government of the day. Margaret Thatcher and her ministers had been outwitted on more than occasion by the cunning of the Gormley-Ezra double act and their ability to defend the conflicting interests of union and management while at the same time combining their efforts to force the government's hands on issues of joint interest.

My first experience of the cordial relations which had previously existed behind the scenes was at the NUM's 1980 annual conference in Eastbourne. On the final evening Sir Derek hosted a dinner at the Grand Hotel, the last but one social gathering of its kind before Ezra and Gormley both retired. Management, union officials and their wives were at ease in each other's company and the fraternising was not without purpose. When the two sides identified a common threat it was usually far easier to agree a joint approach.

Earlier in the week a report to the Eastbourne conference from the union's national executive committee had stressed the importance of the tripartite meetings between the mining unions, board and government over the steps which would have to be taken if the UK was to maintain its ground-breaking work in connection with the future utilisation of coal. Extra state funding was needed to continue experimenting with fluidised-bed combustion and to develop and construct a liquefaction plant at the Point of Ayr colliery in North Wales to turn coal into oil. Tests at Grimethorpe had shown that power station efficiency could be increased by up to fifty per cent if coal was combusted at higher heat rates; the board's scientists had also been experimenting with two methods of turning coal into liquid fuels.

Pioneering work on coal conversion had the NUM's full support and the leadership was at one with the management in trying to make sure that Britain's technical lead was not surrendered to West Germany or the USA. Talks had begun with the government in November 1979 and there had been a further tripartite meeting in February 1980 but it was clear by the conference in the following July, shortly after the publication of the Coal Industry Bill, that the recently-elected Conservative government was intent on reducing state subsidies and on requiring the NCB to break even by 1983-4. In his address to delegates, Sir Derek said that although the Board welcomed a proposed increase in its borrowing limit, the management were concerned about the timetable for phasing out operating grants. He hoped the mining unions would join the board in seeking financial flexibility from the government because the results of research into using coal to produce liquid fuels, chemical feedstock and substitute natural gas were 'stimulating world-wide interest'.

Little did the two sides know that within a few months of their friendly socialising at Eastbourne the coal industry would enter a period of confrontation which would precipitate the 1984-5 strike and put an end to the lofty talk about Britain leading the world in technological advances in the use of coal. Because of mounting concern within the union at the speed with which the government intended to implement what had become the Coal Industry Act, the NUM began talks with leaders of the rail and steel unions to see if it would be possible to revive the triple alliance to fight the impact of retrenchment in their industries.

Then, in January 1981, Joe Gormley's worst fears were confirmed: because of falling demand and the financial stringency imposed by the government, the NCB was told it would have to cut production by ten million tons, requiring the closure of up to 25 pits and the loss of 20,000 jobs, around a tenth of the workforce. Unofficial strike action in South Wales had already spread to other areas and a national stoppage seemed imminent when, on 18 February, Ezra and Gormley led their delegations into the Department of Energy for the latest round of tri-partite talks.

The scene was set for Margaret Thatcher's first and only

U-turn in response to the threat of a miners' strike. On the strength of the guidance given earlier in the day at a Downing Street lobby briefing, industrial and labour correspondents had expected the government to stand firm but to our surprise Gormley emerged from the meeting to announce that David Howell, Secretary of State for Energy, had promised more money for the industry. In my hurried, hand-written script for radio news I said this meant 'that the threat of closure had been withdrawn from every pit'.

Once the scale of the government's retreat sank in and it emerged that the government was ready to add another £300 million to the NCB's cash limit, Ezra and Gormley insisted that this must include funding for the proposed coal liquefaction plant. Finally in June, after weeks of lobbying by the board and union, Howell confirmed that his department would contribute £5 million towards a pilot plant at the Point of Ayr to test methods for converting coal to oil. The following month at the NUM's 1981 conference in Jersey, Ezra announced that with the Department of Energy's support, the NCB had increased its annual budget for research to £50 million and he was confident Britain would continue to lead the world in coal utilisation.

Ezra was as good as his word and despite continuing doubts within the government about the commercial viability of the project, the Board invited tenders in September 1981 for the construction of a £35 million pilot plant to test a liquefaction process which had been pioneered in South Africa and which had been worked on by chemists and engineers at the Coal Research Establishment at Stoke Orchard in Gloucestershire. Twenty-five tonnes of ground-up coal would be mixed with a solvent at high temperatures to produce a form of liquid crude which could then be "cracked" and processed in an oil refinery. The NCB's process had a significant potential advantage over rival technologies in West Germany and the USA and if, by the late 1990s, it became commercially attractive, the Board hoped it would provide a new market for Britain's coal reserves and become a substitute for dwindling supplies of North Sea oil.

Another sign of coal's resurgence was the NCB's £1 billion investment in the new Selby coalfield in Yorkshire which was rapidly becoming a showcase for the world's most advanced mining systems. By the summer of 1980 shaft sinking had been completed at the five pits within the complex and the board predicted that output would reach ten million tons a year and last for thirty years. Selby symbolised the turnaround in the industry. As the president and chairman said their farewells at the 1981 conference, all the talk was of a bright future. Sales had exceeded 117 million tonnes in the preceding twelve months and Gormley believed that if the industry could exploit the newly-developed combustion techniques for more efficient coal-fired generation, they could increase output to 200 million tonnes a year. Ezra pointed to the industry's contribution to the economy: coal had become one of Britain's largest overseas earners, turning over £500 million a year when overseas sales of machinery and technology were taken together with exports of coal and coke.

Britain is no stranger to rapid industrial change and industries have come and gone in the past but nothing bears comparison with the collapse of deep mining for coal and the devastation of the coalfield communities. When conducting research for my proposed programme 'If only...' I had to make the best possible guesstimate of what the industry might have looked like at the 20th anniversary of the strike.

The most upbeat assessment was from Malcolm Edwards, the NCB's commercial director during the strike. If there had been a negotiated settlement, he believed that in 2004 the industry could have still been producing 50 million tons a year with a workforce of 20,000. 'What it needed was a reasonable compromise early on in the strike. If the NUM had agreed to deliver security of supply in return for a four-year pay deal linked to retail prices index, then Thatcher would have settled. It needed a long-term deal'.

Any wishful thinking would have had to be tempered by the grim reality of the lead-up to the privatisation of British Coal. In December 1994, at the chairman's final lunch for industrial correspondents, I sat next to Kevan Hunt, director of employee relations. My note of what he said would have been the pay off to 'If Only...' as it encapsulated the death throes of a once great industry:

'We saw Michael Heseltine in the summer of 1992, just before he announced the closure of 31 pits that October. He refused point blank to stop the dash-for-gas although forty coal-fired power stations had already been closed. The Conservatives dropped the ban on burning gas for generating electricity in 1990. Gas stations are much cheaper to build and are much more profitable...We knew a future Labour government could not do anything because the privatised regional electricity companies cannot be forced to burn coal...I don't think there is any chance of a comeback. Even if coal for oil becomes a proposition, it will be done in Australia where coal reserves are so cheap... We knew the moment we met Heseltine that the coal industry was finished. He said the dash-for-gas had been a great commercial success. We could see Heseltine liked the political freedom it had given the Conservatives. I think he could have saved the industry if only he had been willing to stop the dash for gas'.

The damage done in Scotland
Joe Owens

Already it's 25 years since the strike that has coloured and will, in all its brightness, shades and shadows, influence me until the moment I pass.

I wasn't even 25 years then. Just nineteen. In fact I still regarded people of that, then unfeasible age, to be getting on a bit. I never anticipated the precipitous drop into my own twenties that year would bring.

Anniversaries are, of course, confected. What does one year bring that a previous one didn't or the next promise? But they do focus attention. And if anything in labour and social history deserves reflection and analysis, then it is the 1984 strike.

I will say something on the role of the media during the conflict - and a conflict is what it was - and will tell you just two of many stories of victims I knew that prove that, a small bit later.

Scotland has always been different. But any area of the federated NUM would claim that distinction. As an area, it had an influence disproportionate to its size, an integrity no more special, less or more, but different none the less.

One of the illustrations of that is, when the decision at national level was made to go back to work after the year, on that fateful but proud and defiant Tuesday, we thrawn folk voted to defy it and stay out. Admittedly that defiance only lasted a day but at my then pit, Polkemmet, we had T-shirts with the words 'The Thursday Club' emblazoned on them We were beaten, but not defeated.

By the same token, I was picketing on that Tuesday and tried to stop men who had stayed out for the whole year from going back down, which was their right, it was done. I was young, angry, upset and confused but still realised it was over and had no right to stand before them. I didn't want to let the experience go - but then I had only the burden of my youth to carry.

There is no consolation to be found in this anniversary, nor should sentimentality be allowed to infiltrate. I have written about that moment too many times to say anything startlingly original and I know that every time I am in the company of other miners, as we always maintain we remain, we seek the same seams, cut the same coal.

I was arrested during the strike on the innocuous charge of breach of the peace, normally dealt with by a fine. This time it was different. The court decided to order a social work report. This is crucial - they didn't just want to criminalise a community that was largely self-policing, for good or ill, they wanted to stigmatise it. Another aspect of the carefully thought out strategy to inflict defeat and humiliation. As soon as the social worker knocked on the door, my mother started to cry and ran to the kitchen. The strategy seemed to be working. The woman, who was herself both embarrassed and ashamed to be there but was only following court orders, sat down with me and my father in the living room. We chatted and she took notes. Then my mother came in and sat down, so the social worker asked her a few questions, including 'What would you do if your husband or son went back to their work?' Understand this: me and my father were on strike, there were another five children, all at school, to be cared for, my mother was a part-time cleaner, there was little or no money and only the consideration of the community and strike centre to rely on. She replied: 'I wouldn't have them back in the house.'

That was what summed up to me what the architects of this strategy did not and could not understand, the strength of historical memory. The fibres that come together to create something unbreakable. Beatable, yes. But unbreakable. My mother, the daughter and sister of miners had seen and been through it before. It was bred in the bone. The strategy failed.

There is only room for three people here. Two because I choose, and one because I must. The first is called Sammy. Sam was what is referred to as a character, had all the considerations you require of the stereotypical miner – tall, broad, outspoken, liked a drink, looked after his family, and so on. But the strike broke him and everything he had into the equivalent of what he smashed up his furniture into, firewood for a cold house with nothing left in it. Shattered. Abandoned.

One of my most vibrant memories of the many rallies we had in Glasgow's George Square - an iconic space for such gatherings of the Scottish Labour Movement - is of Sammy climbing on to the open-topped bus the invited speakers were set to deliver their speeches from and say, with arms outstretched, that the miners were being crucified. He was prescient beyond his knowing and having lost his family, died younger than he should.

Another is Jimmy. There was a bus organised to go from our strike centre to Orgreave. Of course, no one knew then what was to be faced. Jimmy had broken his leg and was in plaster, so, in the commotion, when the snatch squads broke out, he couldn't run away. When he was caught, they rebroke his leg. That's the way it was, bitter and rotten. But they broke more.

Jimmy was a gentle man. This is a man who, with his children, used to send Easter cards to his pet rabbits. He died young too.

Then there is another Jimmy. A former leader of the famous shipyard workers' strike in Govan, who morphed into a pseudo intellectual and at the time had a column in then Scotland's biggest selling newspaper. During the strike he used that space to remorselessly attack it, arguing it was undemocratic because there was no ballot. Not an original criticism, I'll agree. He then went on to Channel 4 where, against a black background, he continued his rant. But then there were some things he didn't and couldn't understand.

In Scotland we did have a ballot. At the pit head we had a show of hands on every shift. The pit's NUM delegate took a mandate from that and went to an area meeting where, again, a vote was taken. That happened in every one of the then 14 pits in the area, and every one of the area's 14,000 miners was so consulted. Scotland voted to strike – democratically.

At Bilston Glen, which was used by British Coal as a dumping ground for those who chose to return to work, otherwise known as scabs, and where I ironically ended up becoming the NUM delegate, the canteen windows were smashed during the dispute. Management kept them smashed for a time after we went back to work. For them, it wasn't enough to have the upper hand, they felt they had to be relentless in their retribution.

Then there was the use of haulage firms, such as, infamously, Yuill and Dodds in Scotland. A firm who, when their lorries pass by – a quarter century later - I still cry out 'scab', much to the discombobulation of the others in the car, because they cannot grasp the impact and imprint that year made.

There is a moment that soldiers talk about, the fact that they can only honestly and openly talk about the experiences they've been through with others who have been there. It is the same with the Strike. I can and do talk about it but now there are people untouched by it, to whom it is of no more consequence than an argument they had at work. It is no criticism of them but sometimes it is like shouting in a cave, hearing only an echo.

There are communities in Scotland that will never recover from that time, where too much was taken and little remains. As I write there is a noise about credit crunches and crises. But you can't take anything away from where nothing is.

Having said that, in Denis O'Donnell's poem you will find an evocation of the observation the great Polish poet Czeslow

Milosz made that: 'The purpose of poems is to remind us how difficult it is to remain one person.'

No one person I speak to who has been through that time says anything different. We are different but we are one.

The Miners' Welfare
Bathgate Road, Blackburn

On the road up from the Cross
is the ground where the Miners' stood,
a blasted site, strewn with rubble.
one can pan back through time,
like an archaeological excavation
and observe that, before the Club
was built and razed,
this was the miners' quoiting-green,
levelled for the purpose
by teams of men on summer evenings.

One summer morning in childhood
in a leafy lane I was startled by men
exotic as blackamoors
with lights in their heads,
returning home while a new coffle toiled,
pale as ghosts, in the labyrinths below.

At week-ends, the Miners' detonated into life,
with dancing, drinking and fighting.
There are no miners around here now;
They've been summoned up from darkness
into a world of light.
Where giant wheels pitched against the sky
and where heavy wagons clashed,
all is now sealed and silent as graves.
From these pits there is no resurrection.

Dennis O'Donnell

Twenty five years on: Life on the coalfields of Durham and South Wales
Huw Beynon

On Saturday 12 July 2008 the streets of the City of Durham were filled with the people celebrating the 124th Miners Gala to be held in the area. Amongst the banners being paraded through the city that day was one from the Tower Colliery in South Wales. The cheers of the people followed its path along Silver Street as the knowledgeable crowd recognised the efforts of the men and women who had kept the mine open in common ownership in spite of the efforts of British Coal to close it down. On that day the Tower banner joined many others representing villages whose mines had closed down in the recent and more distant past. Many of these banners were newly-made replicas commissioned by local people and various 'banner groups', often with the assistance of the Lottery Heritage Fund. The Handen Hold mine closed along with many others in Durham in 1968. Its last banner was made in 1961, and its replica, with a portrait of Aneurin Bevan on the front, was a further recognition of the way in which the two coalfields shared a common history and heritage.

Two coal fields, one strike

A delegation from Tower had also marched through Durham in 1983, as part of the Centenary Gala. On that occasion, the air was filled with a strong sense of solidarity, coupled with an anticipation of a struggle that lay ahead. In the previous year, and as part of the NUM's Campaign For Coal, twinning between lodges and the establishment of jointly attended weekend schools had seen the beginnings of a common approach built on shared understandings and close contact. These two coalfields were similar in many ways and both had more than their fair share of tragedy. Mostly this was though mine explosions, the last one at Easington in 1951. But tragedy had also extended beyond the mine, as in Aberfan in 1966 when the waste from the Merthyr Vale colliery killed a whole generation of children. United through their past, the talk in 1983 was of having 'backs against the wall' and the fear of a world without the mine. By 1994 that world had become a reality.

Colliery closures

In 1985 immediately after the strike ended it became clear that the closure programme envisaged by the Board was now far more extensive than that announced in 1984, and admitted to during the strike. Fifty mines were to close and with them 50,000 jobs. During the strike the deputy's (supervisor's) union NACODS balloted its members and 82% voted in favour of strike action to support the miners striking to keep collieries open. Rather than strike, the union negotiated the setting up of a fresh, independent, element to the existing colliery review procedure. In Durham the men at the Horden colliery voted against closure as did those at Bold in Northumberland and St John's in South Wales. The review of Horden supported the decision to close the mine. Bates was next and although the Review concluded that the mine should be kept open, the government supported British Coal in its decision to continue with the closure. By this time St John's had closed along with a swathe of collieries across South Wales.

In writing about the scale of the closures it is common to talk of Two Phases, the first following the strike and another in the early nineties just when it seemed that the industry had stabilised at a lower level. This pattern clearly fits the experience of Durham. The closures in 1985 ended deep mining in the West of the County but left a string of highly mechanised mines operating along the Eastern coast. In South Wales however mines closed annually throughout the eighties. By the time Blaenant closed in 1990, twenty two collieries had closed with four closing in 1989, including the powerful Oakdale mine.

Table one
Decline in mining employment

	1971	1981	1991
South Wales	38,000	25,000	1,200
Durham	22,000	15,000	4,900

Table two
Colliery closures in South Wales and Durham: 1985-1994

	Phase One	*Phase Two*
South Wales	Bedwas (1985)	Blaenant (1990)
	Blaenserchan (1985)	Deep Navigation (1991)
	Celynen South (1985)	Penalta (1991)
	Treforgan Drift (1985)	Taff Merthyr (1992)
	Abertillery (1985)	Betws (1993)
	Celynen North (1985)	Tower (1994)
	Penrhiwchyber (1985)	
	Aberpergwm (1985	
	St Johns (1985)	
	Garw Valley (1985)	
	Maerdy (1986)	
	Cwm (1986)	
	Markham (1986)	
	Nantgarw (1986)	
	Six Bells (1987)	
	Abernant (1988	
	Lady Windsor (1988)	
	Cwnheidre (1989)	
	Marine (1989)	
	Merthyr Vale (1989)	
	Oakdale (1989)	
	Trelewis Drift (1989)	

	Phase One	Phase Two
Durham	Herrington (1985)	Dawdon (1991)
	Sacriston (1985)	Murton/Hawthorn Combine
	Hordon/Blackhall (1986)	(1991)
	Eppleton (1986)	Seaham/Vane Tempest (1992)
		Easington (1993)
		Westoe (1993)
		Wearmouth (1993)

By 1991 mining employment in South Wales had been virtually wiped out. Durham followed as its super-pits along the coast closed down denuding the whole of the Easington District of manual work for men. At that time Betws and Tower remained opened but they too faced the axe with Betws reopening under a management buy-out. After an enormous struggle against the duplicity of the employer the Tower colliery at Hirwaen was taken over by the work-force and kept in production until 2008.

Holding on at Tower

The story of Tower colliery in Hirwaun is well known.It has been celebrated as Opera and in the French cinema. Its fame - stuck out on the northern most scarp on the South Wales coalfield - gave it a kind of celebrity status. It is also seen by many as a beacon of hope; the survival of an idea, of what could be done. It lasted for fourteen years until, finally exhausted, it closed in 2008. In explaining its success, and the commitment of the workforce to the idea, discussions at Tower turned around two critical factors. As pit after pit closed, the men who refused to leave the industry were moved on to other pits. Tower was the last:

'there were hard-core people in Tower who wanted to stay in the mining industry no matter what. Even at their own expense - putting money in themselves. There was a lot of things they could do, they could have let the colliery go and it would have been bought by somebody else like they did in Yorkshire…but you had a hard-core of people here, the most awkward bastards in the British Coalfields - us stuck up here in Tower!' Dai Dosco observed.

The period when the mine was to be closed remains highly charged in the memory of these men. The leadership cadre remember the details of the events, the drama of the decision and the evocative sense of achievement that surrounded the successful purchase of the mine. Glyn Rogers remembers how:

'The first year was under ownership when everybody was walking on air because at least one-third of the men had been outside in the big bad world, on the dole, and the other two-thirds had actually been working in low paid jobs in a factory on the production line and they had to put their hand up to go to the toilet and various other things so they didn't like the outside world and they realised that… it is a lot easier to work in a colliery without somebody standing over you.'

This account of factory work, its tedium and regulation, was a common one, and often linked to ideas of mutual support and solidarity. One man puts it like this:

'And you stood together. But if you go outside and what have you, you'll see men struggling on their own. Underground you wouldn't see a man struggle, you wouldn't have to ask anybody to give you hand, they should automatically see you struggling and they come and give you a hand.'

This reference to the quality of alternative employment, the low level of wages and associated levels of tedium crop up repeatedly in the account that these men gave of their reasons for 'taking a chance' in 1994.

The problem of mining communities

The Report on the closure of the Horden Colliery in 1985 noted that:

'Serious consequences will result in the local community if (the colliery) is closed, not only on adult employment and youth employment but on the economy generally'.

This proved to be the case and the state of the coal districts became a major issue in the 1997 election. Labour in opposition had not fought the closure of mines but rather argued for the economic regeneration of the mining districts. As such one of the first acts of John Prescott's Department was to set up a Task Force to enquire into the condition of life on the coalfields. Its conclusions on the scale of 'deprivation and decline' in these areas as well as their 'unique combination of concentrated joblessness, physical isolation, poor infrastructure and severe health problems'[1] were widely reported. The findings of the Taskforce built upon research that had been conducted by the Coalfields Communities Campaign that had charted the impact of the post 1992 closures on specific coal mines. Generally a pattern emerged of 'pensioning off' though various kinds of benefit and - for the economically active ex-miners – an average reduction in wages of £100 per week. Furthermore it became clear that in these mining places exceptionally high proportions of the labour force were on disability benefit. A statistical analysis of mining wards in England published by the Department for the Regions demonstrated that the 'coal district' impact was discernable twenty years after the closure of the mine:

'We concluded that health suffered a systematic casual relationship with an area's past history in mining, but was intimately linked with other basic measures of socio-economic well-being at the local level in these same parts of the country'.[2]

By the mid to late nineties the fact that there was a problem in the old coalfield districts was incontestable. The Indices of

Deprivation, published by the DETR indicated that no less that 63.5% of coalfield wards were amongst the 20% most deprived of England across the whole span of multiple indices. The Welsh data reveal a similar pattern with the majority of the country's most deprived wards being located in the old coalfield districts. Repeatedly, as examples of poverty or neglect were sought by the media it was toward South Wales and the North East that it turned - most commonly to Merthyr, Blaenau Gwent and Easington.

At the turn of the century in South Wales and Durham the old mining areas stood out as having very low proportions of the labour force in work, low levels of wages, high incidence of limiting long term illness, poor housing and poor patterns of educational attainment. These features are compounded in particular places by high incidences of crime and drug abuse. Comparing Easington with Rhondda Cynon Taff for example at that time we find that both places demonstrated a population growth of well below that of the UK average. In both places, young men and women in the 15-29 age group were leaving to find work elsewhere. For those who remained the percentage of births outside marriage was well above the average for England and Wales, and the number of births to women under the age of twenty was significantly higher than the national average. Both places had well above average proportions of people on housing benefit, and high levels of household poverty.

Growth but still marginal and prone to injury

The current financial crisis raises in dramatic terms the weakness of the market in correcting major imbalances. The closures of the coal mines, with the removal of almost half a million high-wage jobs was an equally dramatic example, but much less well reported and discussed. At the time of the strike, free marketers talked of labour locked into unproductive jobs by state support. Once freed, it was argued, a swath of productive economic activity would emerge on the coalfields. British Coal's Enterprise scheme talked of replacing all of the jobs with new high-waged employment. After twenty years, research from Sheffield Hallam University indicated that no more than 47% of these 'lost' jobs had been 'replaced' in coalfield districts.[3]

During Gordon Brown's boom years new employment did come to the coalfield districts but this was not achieved by the guiding hand of the market. As the scale of the economic problems increased the level of public funds devoted to coalfield regeneration increased incrementally. This involved the enormous efforts of local authorities, various schemes from Europe (including Objective One for the whole of the South Wales Coalfield and most of Yorkshire), the British Government (SRB, Selective Area Status, Enterprise Zones, etc), the Welsh Assembly (Communities First), English Heritage (a government funded agency), the Lottery, and latterly the Coalfield Regeneration Trust and Save the Children. The total amount of public funding that has been used in an attempt to compensate for the loss of mining employment has been enormous. In 2004 Dave Feickert, put the figure at: 'at least £28bn. This is nearly half of the North Sea tax revenues of £60bn collected since 1985.'[4]

What had became clear was that the coalfields were forced to compete for a limited flow of new manufacturing and service projects with urban centres and other more favoured sites. Equally clear was the fact that some coalfields were better placed than others to attract such investment, and that each in turn would be affected by the local as well as the national context. As a result the central coalfield areas of England have been better placed than those in the North East and South Wales to benefit from the boom. In Durham for example, where there has been significant success in attracting jobs for men to the Eastern corridor along the A19, many of these jobs have been taken by people commuting from outside of the old coal districts. In South Wales new employment has tended to grow along the corridor of the M4 motorway with limited job opportunities along the Northern rim of the old coalfield. Here commuting is in the other direction, taking people out of the coalfield areas. As the financial crisis bites unemployment rates in Durham and South Wales were the first to show steep rises. Across both areas more than one in ten men of working age remain on disability benefit; in some places it is as high as one in two.

History fights back

Talking at Durham in 2008, Tyrone O'Sullivan reflected with sadness on the closure of Tower but with pride over their achievement and the demonstration of 'the way ordinary people can stand up for themselves and change the world'. Increasingly ideas like these are harder to hold on to. Incrementally, in Durham and South Wales, there has been a shift in political perceptions. As mining became seen as a thing of the past, a change of emphasis has developed into a real forgetting. But in these places history has a way of fighting back. The Gala continues and is much more than the tourist spectacle some envisaged. In South Wales the global demand for coking coal has led Tata, the owners of Corus, to contemplate a new drift mine employing up to 700 miners, linked to the Port Talbot steel works.

Notes

1   Task Force

2   DETR, 2003

3   Christine Beatty, Stephen Fothergill, and Ryan Powell, *Twenty Years On: Has the Economy of the Coalfields Recovered?* paper presented at Regional Studies Association Conference, Aalborg, 2005

4   D. Feickert, 'Arthur was right by instinct' *The Guardian*, 2004

Trade unions, public relations and the media
Paul Routledge

It was the biggest event of their lives, and the biggest story of my life. It was a privilege to be present at the Miners' Revolt, which is what it was, not just a strike, but it was also a harrowing experience, and an object lesson in the reality of power politics.

1984-85 demonstrated the pivotal function of the media, but also exposed the weakness of trade union public relations and the flawed assumptions that flowed from decades of remarkably close contacts between leaders of the National Union of Mineworkers and sections of the press. When the sledgehammer came down, a lot of journalists got out of the way.

Have the media lessons of the strike been learned? Indeed, what are they? Do the unions do it better now? What happened to those who still write about these issues? Where did the audience go? Was there really an audience in the first place? Have the media managers and the proprietors written the labour movement out of the picture? And is there enough bitter in the club cellar to fuel this debate?

We have to ask these questions now, because we didn't think to do so at the time. The rush of events, the adrenalin of deadlines, stilled any doubts. The din of newsdesks clamouring for copy drowned out questioning voices. A quarter of a century later, we have a duty to seek answers.

For many years, long before I became a labour correspondent for *The Times* in 1969, there existed a rapport between NUM leaders like Arthur Horner, Sid Ford and Will Paynter and senior industrial correspondents on Fleet Street. The NUM was always a 'Number One's' preserve, jealously guarded.

Later generations continued that close contact. Barrie Devney of the *Daily Express* was privy to the thoughts of Joe Gormley. In fact, I suspect he originated quite a lot of them, though Joe had no rival for guile. Mick Costello of the *Morning Star* and I were close to Lawrence Daly, and latterly, Mick McGahey. We drank with the Left members of the executive after their (officially secret) pre-executive conclave in the County Hotel, Bloomsbury.

Every summer, usually in the first week of July, at least a couple of dozen journalists attended the miners' annual conference, known informally as The Drinkathlon. And every paper covered the monthly post-executive briefing at 222 Euston Road. We usually repaired to the pub with EC members – the Left and Right (invariably referred to in the media as 'moderates') had different watering holes. Some became personal friends.

This was also true lower down the chain of command in the NUM. A conference week at seaside resorts like Aberdeen, Morecambe, Jersey (Joe Gormley's favourite), Tenby, Inverness, Tynemouth, and much to my pleasure, Scarborough, brought us into close proximity with branch delegates, secretaries and ordinary working miners. We learned much from them. They had - indeed, still have - a marvellous story to tell. We warmed to it, and them.

And not just us. Readers have always had a soft spot for miners. I think they had an instinctive sympathy for men who risk their lives so they can switch on the lights. I well remember in 1990, when Tory Industry Secretary Michael Heseltine announced the butchery of the coal industry, a self-confessed 'natural' Tory voter, Paula Radford, of Leeds, wrote to her local paper asking : 'What can I do to fight this? I will write, picket, anything. Please help me and other little people to stop this happening.' Other images: a middle-aged, middle class woman in leafy Hertfordshire crying into the sink while washing the dishes. The waxed jacket and pearly earring demonstrators in Cheltenham. Happily, some things are beyond spin. This was, though it didn't save the pits. Not a penny of the £760 million eventually set aside by a government shocked by public reaction was ever spent on keeping the collieries going.

If this historic relationship between the miners, their union and the media sounds too cosy, it probably was. But it worked for both sides, if not always to the satisfaction of editors who thought we were too close. We got the stories - which after the successful strikes of 1972 and 1974 were much sought after - and they got the publicity. In retrospect, probably too much.

All that changed in 1984, when practically all the newspapers and much of radio and TV hastened into an alliance with the Thatcher government. In the face of a perceived insurrection, the Third and Fourth Estates closed ranks. Thereafter, and increasingly as the strike grew more bitter and violent (on both sides), the media played a role substantially supportive of the establishment. On occasions, it went even further, intervening directly. *The Times* gave space to David Hart, an entrepreneur organising and funding the working miners' groups.

The camaraderie that had existed between Fleet Street and NUM leaders counted for virtually nothing. From the editors' point of view, it was expendable in wartime. Arthur Scargill was no longer welcome in the Gray's Inn Road directors' dining room of Times Newspapers, as he once was. At the same time, Scargill and his cohorts withdrew much of the liaison that had previously existed, dealing increasingly with fewer and fewer media favourites. Press relations practically collapsed, and the government-Coal Board propaganda machine had far too free a rein in the media. This had industrial consequences. A daily diet of TV coverage of men breaking the strike unquestionably accelerated the return to work.

The strike also threw up some tough calls for newspapers. One sticks in my mind most memorably. In October 1984, members of the pit deputies' union NACODS voted by 82 per cent to join the NUM strike. Without them, no pit could operate legally. The entire industry faced shutdown. The ballot result was declared at NACODS headquarters in Doncaster. There was jubilation among miners, who scented victory.

I was drinking with strikers in the Danum hotel, and phoned *The Times* nightdesk at around 10 p.m. to check all was well and ask what the splash story was. It was the NACODS event, but not the strike prospect story I had filed. Our correspondent in Birmingham had later, well-founded information that deputies at the pits still working - particularly Nottinghamshire and the Midlands - would not abide by their own union's strike ballot. New, accurate story always trumps old story, no matter whom it hurts. That is a cruel lesson, best learned early in any conflict. I remember going back to the bar, where the tape was playing to Cyndi Lauper's *Time After Time*, to tell my friends the unpalatable truth. It has always been my view that the strike was lost that day. Thatcher dreamed up a 'solution' to buy off NACODS, Scargill spurned this settlement and the rest is history.

In the end, public relations disappeared in the gunsmoke of power relations. No amount of publicity, even favourable, could hold back the juggernaut of a government with quasi-wartime police controls. A similar - bleaker, even - picture unfolded during the Wapping dispute that followed very soon after. The print unions had very few friends in the media. I was one of them, and paid the price with my job during the dispute. By contrast, Rupert Murdoch had many allies in an establishment now practised in the skills of putting down rebellion.

That was the demoralised setting inherited by the labour movement in the late 1980s. But there were stirrings, particularly in public sector unions, of a refashioning of media relations on a more professional footing. Instead of pints in the pub with an old-timer general secretary, it might be a briefing from an enthusiastic young press officer. Indeed, it might even be a woman. Unheard of. Of course there was no abrupt transition from one style to another. Older journalists still tended to rely on private chats with full-time officials. Younger reporters, more used to the PR era (which came late to this field) were happy to get their information from the press office. Like talks to like.

The theory that good public relations can win struggles was put to the test in the ambulance workers' dispute of 1989-90, and found wanting. The National Union of Public Employees, with tireless Lynne Bryan (a professional refugee from the Engineering Employers' Federation) at the publicity wheel, won the PR campaign but lost the war to a cunning, and ultimately more powerful, Tory Health Secretary in the shape of Ken Clarke.

That setback did not halt the rise and rise of the union media machine, however. Whether it was simply a matter of catching up with the rest of society, or a conscious decision to follow Churchill's dictum of jaw, jaw rather than war, war, the unions sought increasingly to do battle with words and pictures rather than placards and pickets. As the strike rate fell, the impetus towards public persuasion gathered strength. It continues to do so.

In 1968, when I started on the industrial beat in London, there were around 70 labour and industrial correspondents working for the newspapers, news agencies, radio and TV. Most national dailies had at least three. The Times, which I joined in 1969, at one time had four in London and three more in the regions. But very few unions had press officers. The TUC had one - chain-smoking, seen-it-all Bob Hartwell. Jack Jones, general secretary of the TGWU, spoke directly to the press. Every industrial correspondent had his home phone number. And that of Lawrence Daly, the NUM's canny general secretary; unfortunately, he was rarely at home.

Fast forward forty years, and the number of trade unionists has halved to 6.5 million. The labour correspondent is an endangered species. I can think of only two left, on the Press

Association and the *Financial Times*. Yet there are dozens of media officers in the labour movement. A perverse form of Parkinson's Law is at work, which requires the number of trade union spin doctors to rise in inverse proportion to the number of ears they have to bend. At last year's [2008] Trades Union Congress, I counted 49 union press officers, with nine from the TUC itself.

Fortunately for them, their role has changed. The TUC's press office is now the 'campaigns and communications' department, with a much wider brief that the days of old Bob Hartwell. Unions realise that in an era where membership has tumbled dramatically, and their role in society has diminished, they have to shout louder to make their voice heard. The trend away from traditional heavy industries towards smaller workplaces in hi-tech industries, with fewer employees has made it much harder to recruit new members - the lifeblood of any union - on the shopfloor. Prospective members are also wooed through the media, through positive stories about campaigns ranging from bread and butter issues like pay to contemporary problems such collapsing pension funds, maternity and paternity rights, health and safety and the work-life balance. For public sector unions, maintaining services, particularly the NHS, is a key issue that affects everyone, not just union members, but it also sustains the profile of a union like Unison.

These lines of activity are crucial for every union, including the NUM. In recent years, with the partial retirement of Arthur Scargill, the miners' voice has not been heard so strongly. That is a pity. More than a pity, it is letting down the men and their families. Under Ken Capstick, the union is once again producing an excellent magazine on events affecting miners and their industry. There is also a first-rate website, www.num. org.uk, which keeps internet users up to date. There ought to be more.

And personal relations still count. A year ago, I was invited to an NUM weekend school to talk about the unions and the media. I was happy to accept and do my stuff, but the event swiftly deteriorated into a slanging match over my unauthorised - and unflattering - biography of Scargill, published sixteen years previously.

Disappointing. That war is over. Nothing is gained by remaining in the trenches of 1984, powerful though those experiences and memories are. The NUM has a new general secretary, Chris Kitchen, from Kellingley colliery. I believe he would like to break out of the stranglehold of the past. There are more pressing issues, like the battle to gain recognition at Hatfield colliery and others that may come on stream now that the international price of coal is so high. Media exposure is part of that battle.

That is one of the lessons of the strike that has been inadequately learned. You cannot rest in the endeavour to tell the members and the public what's going on, and why. It may not win every strike, or your favourite campaign but it is part and parcel of modern trade unionism. If it were unnecessary, why would the employers, their trade associations and the government hire so many media people? Whitehall departments alone have more information officers than there are miners in Britain.

Perhaps I may be allowed to end on a personal note. When the Moloch of the workplace, Rupert Murdoch, came for us at Wapping, I was a foreign correspondent for *The Times*, covering South East Asia from a base in Singapore. I had been sent there very soon after the Great Strike, in May 1985, principally as a means of getting me out of my job as Labour Editor, which I had held for fifteen years. I was regarded as too close to the unions, and certainly too close to the miners. And that was probably a correct political judgment.

Anyway, I was in Manila, capital of the Philippines, covering the downfall of the hated President Marcos when the bomb dropped in Gray's Inn Road in January 1986: go to Wapping and scab with the renegade printers supplied by the strike-breaking EETPU, or get the sack. I phoned my wife and asked her what she thought I should do. She told me to do what I thought was right. I thought a bit further and rang John Stones, NUM delegate at Frickley colliery in South Elmsall, in the south Yorkshire coalfield and asked him what I should do. His reply was unforgettable: 'If you're ringing me, you know already.'

That was enough. I never wrote another word for *The Times*, and was first suspended without pay and then sacked after five months, along with another dozen or so colleagues on the paper – including the entire Labour Staff of Donald Macintyre, David Felton and Barrie Clement, all 'day oners' like me. The public world of industrial journalism had come full circle with my private life. I don't regret it, indeed I still drink with the lads of Frickley colliery, which closed in 1992. Recently I was made a member of the village's Brookside working men's club.

So you see this is not entirely about the power of the media. It is about people, too. People talking to people, and persuading them. There is no guarantee of success if you do, only a guarantee of failure if you don't.

Afterword
Coal and Climate Change

Coal continues to grab the headlines, both in the UK and internationally.

In China seventy per cent of the nation's energy comes from coal which is fuelling the economic boom, but at enormous environmental and human cost. High levels of air pollution are estimated to cause between 350,000-400,000 premature deaths each year and between five and six thousand workers are killed each year in China's coal mines.

Jeff Goodell's *Big Coal* provides an excellent account of how coal, the fuel of the industrial revolution, has emerged again as 'the default fuel of choice' in the United States. More than 25 percent of the world's recoverable coal reserves – about 270 billion tons – are buried within its borders and within weeks of taking office in January 2000 Bush began staffing regulatory agencies with former coal industry executives and lobbyists, and Vice President Dick Chency's National Energy Policy Development Group's recommendations included building up to 1,900 new power plants over twenty years, a $2 billion, ten-year subsidy for clean coal technology, and a recommendation that the Department of Justice review enforcement actions against dirty coal burners.[1] True to form, in the final month of his presidency Bush also relaxed rules on the disposal of mountain top waste by mine operators in the Appalachians. In mountaintop removal, coal operators use explosives to blow up mountaintops to uncover coal reserves. Leftover rock and dirt – the stuff that used to be the mountains -- is dumped into nearby valleys, burying streams. A government study published in 2003 found that mine operators had buried 724 miles of Appalachian streams between 1985 and 2001

All of this has strengthened the opposition of climate change activists to burning coal and placed the NUM at the centre of fierce debate in the UK. Protests near Drax power station by activists in June and August 2008, and the climate camp near Kingsnorth power station, also in August, to oppose plans to build a new coal-fired power station there, spurred the NUM to produce issues of *The Miner* for the NUM and TUC conferences and a special edition 'in response to the recent spate of protest by the Climate Camp against coal power stations, coal consumption and production'. The NUM's policy acknowledges the catastrophic impact of impending climate change and argues that 'a solution to the man-made impact on the planet's behaviour must be found…We believe seriously, at least when addressing the impact of COAL on this process, clean coal technologies are the most rapid and efficient measures to be deployed'. The union fiercely rejects the slogans used by climate camp protesters ('Leave It In The Ground', 'No Place In Britain's Energy Supply For Coal') and the stance of Greenpeace which has dismissed clean coal technology in a policy document, *False Hope*.[2] The union also takes a global perspective, arguing that worldwide coal reserves will be exploited and coal production will rise from 4 billion tonnes now to 7 billion in twenty year's time. The real task is to develop clean coal technology, carbon capture and storage development globally: 'We are part of the struggle to save the planet, not part of the problem' whereas the climate camp protestors exhibit 'a classic example of utopian thinking'.[3]

The NUM has energetically defended its position, with Arthur Scargill speaking at the Kingsnorth Climate Camp in August , and also, along with North East NUM speakers, at a lively conference, Class, Climate Change & Clean Cole, organised by David Douglass in Newcastle in November 2008 (fig30).

The case for coal, and a new energy policy which recognises the importance of serious research and investment in clean coal technology, is growing stronger. Such a case has to be part a more sustainable, efficient and diverse energy mix, but a number of factors make it urgent.

Firstly we have the worst financial crisis since the Great Depression, caused by the rush for easy profits of commercial and investment banks, hedge funds, insurance companies, private equity firms and other financial institutions. They were able to do this because governments and regulators retreated from any attempt to oversee or check financial excess. Freeing up the markets, and policies driven by deregulation, privatisation and liberalisation, have defined the world economic order since the mid- 1970s.

The impact of these changes, in terms of energy policy for the UK, was to thwart the development of renewable energy and stop the development of cleaner coal technologies which, through increased thermal efficiency, consume much less energy. Dave Feikert, previously with the NUM and now an energy consultant, points out that 'Since 1979 the UK has not had an energy policy. And now it is almost too late'.

Conservative governments closed access to the nation's coal reserves and sped up the depletion of UK gas reserves by burning them in power stations whilst New Labour believed that market forces would manage effectively our energy strategy. Feikert points out, 'But in the long run, as we all know, the market is a moron. It does not order expensive wind turbines, costly nuclear power plants or sink big new coal mines, especially in a private system where electricity regulations set profitability (price) as the key criterion'.[4]

A swathe of the UK power generating industry has been snapped up since privatisation by companies like the French state-owned EDF or the world's largest power and gas company, the German company E.ON. Sharon Beder, in a study of the experience of electricity liberalisation and privatisation in several countries, listed market failures, which led to broken promises regarding price cuts, service and reliability, reducing government deficits and on the environment.[5]

The second important issue which highlights the need for

stable, secure energy is the vulnerability of UK and European energy supply highlighted by the decision by the Russian government in January 2009, in its feud with Ukraine, to shut down pipelines which provide Europe's principal supply of natural gas. The move meant that in the middle of a sharp winter cold spell several European countries were without heat causing schools and factories to close. Gazprom, Russia's powerful state-dominated gas monopoly owns both Russia's gas fields and the pipelines that bring that gas to markets. Gazprom is also closely involved with state-run press and television in Russia which are loyal and powerful mouthpieces for the government. In addition Gazprom's vast revenues enabled it to purchase large equity stakes in energy companies such as ENI in Italy, BASF in Germany and Gaz de France.

The European Union, despite its status as the world's largest economy, has very little in the way of indigenous energy resources and is heavily dependent on Russian oil, gas and coal exports. Thirty per cent of the EU's gas is supplied by Russia, and a similar percentage of Russian coal is used in UK power generation because, in a crazy example of how the market works, UK-mined coal is sold at prices determined by long-term contracts which are less than the delivered cost of imported coal and at levels which do not allow new investment in deep mines.

So the case for coal is boosted because it can be supplied with minimum political or economic risk. But it will require the political will, long-term investment and a commitment to research, develop and install clean coal technology to make it a reality.

Notes

1   Jeff Goodell, *Big Coal: The Dirty Secret Behind America's Energy Future*.
New York: Houghton Mifflin. 2006

2   *The Miner*, Special edition, August 2008, p 1

3   Ibid, pp 2-3

4   Letter in *Financial Times*, 28 April 2005.

5   Sharon Beder, *Powerplay – the Fight to Control the Wworld's Electricity*,
The New Press: New York 2003 pp 325-233

Contributors

Michael Bailey is Senior Lecturer in Media History and Cultural Theory at Leeds Metropolitan University. He is the editor of *Narrating Media History*, Routledge. 2008.

Huw Beynon is Professor and Director of the School of Social Sciences at Cardiff University. He edited *Digging Deeper: Issues in the Miners' Strike*, Verso. 1985, and has since researched the impact of pit closures upon miners, their wives, partners and children and upon coal mining communities.

Andy Boag lives in West Yorkshire and has been photographing for 15 years. The miners' photographs grew out of an MA project at Bolton University and they have now been acquired for the national archive by the National Coal Mining Museum

Tony Harcup is Senior Lecturer in Journalism at the University of Sheffield, and the author of *Journalism: Principles and Practice* (2nd ed. 2009) and *The Ethical Journalist* (2006)

Patricia Holland is a writer, researcher and Senior Lecturer at Bournemouth University. She has worked as a television editor and producer and has published widely in the fields of television, visual culture and popular media. Her most recent book is *The Angry Buzz: 'This Week' and Current Affairs Television*, I.B.Tauris, 2006. She is vice-chair of the Campaign for Press and Broadcasting Freedom.

Nicholas Jones was labour correspondent for BBC Radio News. He won two awards for his coverage of the 1984-5

pit dispute: he was named industrial journalist of the year by the Industrial Society and presented with the annual 'golden bollock' by his colleagues in the labour and industrial correspondents group for having reported in early February 1985 that the strike could be 'over within days' on the strength of a leak from the South Wales NUM that there might be a return to work without an agreement. In fact the strike lasted for another four weeks. He is the author of *Strikes and the Media* (1986).

Peter Lazenby joined the *Wharfedale Observer* in Otley in 1967 as a trainee reporter, aged 17. He joined the *Yorkshire Evening Post* in 1972 and became Industrial Correspondent in 1974. He has been Father of the Chapel for the National Union of Journalists at the *Yorkshire Evening Post* for most of the last 25 years and chair of Leeds NUJ for fifteen years.

Dennis O'Donnell works in West Lothian. He has published two books of poetry: *Two Clocks Ticking* (1998), which won the Saltire Prize for the best first book of the year, and *Smoke and Mirrors* (2003).

Joe Owens was a miner and is now a writer.

Julian Petley is Professor of Film and Television at Brunel University and chair of the Campaign for Press and Broadcasting Freedom.

Robin Ramsay is the editor of *Lobster* and co-authored *Smear! Wilson and the Secret State with Steve Dorril* (1991). A collection of his talks, Politics and Paranoia, was published in 2008.

Paul Routledge is a *Daily Mirror* columnist and was previously political correspondent on *The Observer* and the *Independent on Sunday* and labour editor of *The Times*.

Hilary Wainwright edits *Red Pepper* and is Research Director of the New Politics Programme at the Transnational Institute.

Ken Wilkinson started work at Askern Colliery, near Doncaster, in 1974. The pit closed in 1991. Ken now works as a photographer for the West Yorkshire Fire Service

Granville Williams lives in West Yorkshire and is the author of *Remembering How It Was: A History of Mining in Leeds*. He is on the Campaign for Press and Broadcasting Freedom National Council.

Support the
Campaign for Press and Broadcasting Freedom
Media reform: Still a burning issue
25 years after the miners' strike

The Campaign for Press and Broadcasting (CPBF) was set up thirty years ago, in the aftermath of the massive attack by the national press on trades unions during the 'winter of discontent'. A number of strikes, mainly by low-paid public sector workers, during the winter of 1978-79 became the focus for sustained and grossly exaggerated anti-union reporting and editorial comment. The result of newspaper coverage, amplified in broadcast news, was a powerful shift in public opinion against trades unions which propelled Margaret Thatcher into power in May 1979.

Called the Campaign for Press Freedom when it was launched in 1979 around a founding document *Towards Press Freedom*, it changed its name to the CPBF In 1982 to tackle the deregulatory broadcasting policies being developed by the Conservative government.

We have witnessed dramatic changes in the media since 1979 but the need for a strong, well-supported media reform group is as urgent now as it was during the miners' strike. Then the CPBF argued and campaigned for polices to promote diverse, democratic and accountable media, and the right of reply to inaccurate or biased reporting. It still does.

The policy issues the CPBF is active on are:

● Media ownership and regulation.

The CPBF is currently involved in a major research project *Media Ownership in the Age of Convergence* to develop policies on media ownership.
The importance of this issue is exemplified by one proprietor who has

utilised the political influence his expanding media power confers. Rupert Murdoch acquired *The Times* and *Sunday Times* in 1981 to add to The Sun and The *News of the World* he had owned since 1969. The bitter industrial dispute at Wapping in January 1986 led to the end of newspaper publishing in Fleet Street but the important outcome for Murdoch was that his newspapers began to generate the fabulous profits which enabled him to build his global media group, News Corporation.

Sky TV was launched in 1989, and in November 1990 the satellite competitor BSB merged and BSkyB built up a powerful and unassailable position on this new media platform. In November 2006 BSkyB moved to take a controversial 17.9% stake in ITV.

In September 2006 *thelondonpaper* was launched to compete with Associated Newspapers *London Lite* and the *Evening Standard*. Company accounts reveal that losses of £17 million were incurred by Murdoch in the first ten months of operation, but his intervention to disrupt the London newspaper market was successful. In January 2009 the Russian billionaire Alexander Lebedev acquired a 75.1% stake in the *Evening Standard* for a reported £1.

Rupert Murdoch's role in UK politics – supporting both the Conservative governments of Margaret Thatcher and those of New Labour's Tony Blair – has been detrimental to the democratic process. As an unaccountable and unelected powerful media owner he has influenced UK governments on a range of policies, most notably over Europe but also, crucially, in the support of all of the newspapers in his global media group for the policies pursued by George Bush and Tony Blair leading to the invasion of Iraq in March 2003.

● Public service broadcasting

There has been an explosion of TV mainly through the arrival of cable, satellite and digital TV channels, most of which are subscription or advertising funded. In 2007 there were 470 TV channels which broadcast in the UK, transmitting 2.1 million hours of programming. About one million hours of this output was devoted to shopping, movies, 'adult' and 'other' programming.

BSkyB revenue from subscriptions was more than £3.7 billion in the twelve months to June 2007 whereas the BBC received £.3.3 billion from the licence fee. Apart from the impartiality requirement for Sky News, BSkyB has no regulatory obligations and creates very little original programming, whereas the BBC, as a public service broadcaster, produces a range of news, current affairs, educational, arts as well as comedy, soaps, drama, sport, films and light entertainment on television, radio and the internet. The problem is, in an increasingly commercial television environment, channels such as ITV want to jettison their public service obligations. There is an intense debate on the future of public service broadcasting in the multi-channel digital age

The CPBF believes that public service broadcasting has a vital role to play in our society. A strong, well-funded BBC has to have competition from other public service broadcasters and how we achieve this is a crucial policy issue.

The CPBF has produced several pamphlets on public service broadcasting and responded to numerous consultations from the regulator Ofcom and the Department of Media, Culture and Sport.

● The impact of the internet on traditional media

In the United States the impact of the internet on newspaper advertising and journalists' jobs has been savage, and the UK newspaper industry is now grappling with the fact that newspaper revenue and circulation are declining as readers migrate to the web for information.

The internet is a transforming technology, allowing people to send and receive information and images instantaneously from around the world, but many of the same issues and policy questions connected with traditional media need to be addressed. Who controls the internet, and how should it be regulated? What is the role, value and impact of citizen journalism and user-generated content?

There is also a public policy issue to ensure access for all to the information society by eliminating the digital divide between those with the resources to access the internet and those excluded through poverty and inequality.

Again these are issues which the CPBF is active on, presenting our ideas and arguments in *Free Press*, public debates and consultation responses.

Help Us To Be Effective. Join the CPBF

If you don't think we get the media we deserve, join with us to campaign for more diverse, democratic and accountable media. We are a membership-based organisation which relies on individuals and organisations for the funds to continue to do our work. You can find out more about us and download a membership form from: http://www.cpbf.org.uk, email us at freepress@cpbf.org.uk, write to us at 23 Orford Road, Walthamstow, London E17 9NL, or ring 0208 521 5932.